Soul To Pay

So, Shall I Add Tenfold Thereto

Jay D Stephens

ACKNOWLEDGMENTS

WE ACKNOWLEDGE GOD THE FATHER, JESUS THE SON, AND THE PRECIOUS HOLY SPIRIT IN THIS BLESSED MINISTRY. WE THANK CECILIA, CHRISTINA, JAMES JR., JARED, MOTHER, SISTERS, BROTHER, AND COUSINS, FOR LOVE AND SUPPORT. MAY GOD CONTINUE TO BLESS MY PASTOR AND FIRST LADY; MINISTRIES, MEMBERS, AND FRIENDS. WE HONOR THE MEMORY OF THOSE WHO HAVE PAVED A WAY FOR US AND LESSENED THE ARDUOUS PATH TO SUCCESS. MAY GOD GET THE GLORY.

TABLE OF CONTENTS

Soul to Pay   "...So, Shall I Add Tenfold Thereto"

Introduction

The little brown round-faced boy could not have been any more than five years of age. He raced home with a goal to spend his first half-hour after school doing his homework, and he finished it in record time as usual. He had learned to study harder than others because he wanted to show his appreciation to his parents; and his studying paid off as he was the top student in his class.

As he walked the twenty yards of grass and dirt-road that separated him from his home, he noticed the 'white' angel that stood motionless by the bushes.

Vee was high-yellow with long black hair and she always smiled; including times when she was confused and angry. The little boy knew that she was waiting for him.

"You're my brother," she spoke in a matter of fact tone. She had said this before but it seemed as if the boy was finally old enough to understand it now. He thought, *what does she mean, I'm her brother?*

The boy went to his mother and asked the same question.

"She's telling the truth, Jay; she is your sista'; her mother is your mother." The boy walked away thinking about the ramifications of such a statement. He didn't ask any more questions for fear of what the answer would be. He was satisfied with his old mother being his old mother and keeping things the same. But it made him more uncomfortable to see sisters who were formally cousins with a new mother who was formally an aunt, as he had been told. Although confusing, the revelation helped him when the other boys in the neighborhood would pick with him and call him 'adopted.'

African Americans in the United States have been adopted. The almost angelic voice of opportunity whispers to us: You belong here; you are my brothers and sisters. In the aforementioned story, the boy spent a great deal of time with his great-uncle's family and it made sense for him to not return to a struggling mother. It made sense for a people who had adopted American ways and culture (originally as a subgroup) to remain with the 'new family.'

Having all of the legal rights and benefits of being adopted members of the family, the descendants are considered family members without the stigma or nomenclature of being adopted. And knowing our adopted status, we worked harder than most; and made great contributions under duress.

Yet, the fact remains, family history still leaves some residue in the hearts and minds of the old and new family members. We may have been adopted but there were other adopted family members who contributed less but based on kinship, expect more.

In the Great Melting Pot that is America, all adoptions are final regardless of how we became members of the family. Different factions within the 'pot' have no right to rise up against other groups because everyone has contributed to the country and the country performs better as a unified whole. The boy in the initial story learned family ways and felt more like a brother to two brothers who were previously adopted.

As modern times challenge our principles and whittle away at a trumped up but unstable moral code, those who practice high moral standards are almost considered odd. Emotions and personal beliefs spurred on by personal faith, experiences, and/or insecurities, almost appear as glitches in society's immoral steamroller that seeks to pretend everything in life is flat and even. So, while some are more moral than others; those who refuse to be defined by their morality point the finger of intolerance at those who relish definition by their godly moral code.

Don't hate on me because I am different and I believe in God. Don't take my direction by a profoundly significant doctrine as something that is not fair to all people.

Those proudly living the immoral life will easily sustain the convoluted sinner; especially when he or she professes single-mindedness and fairness as a lifestyle. Those proudly living the lukewarm moral life easily accept the exceptions of the immoral because to them, it makes little difference. In the face of an ever-changing society, the moral high-minded people, who wanted to promote goodness and right, now face the scrutiny of their real beliefs. Some take the high-road and consider acceptance of the deviancy of society as being lenient and fair-minded.

We seek to get along at the cost of losing ourselves. But that is almost a rule of a melting pot republic...you compromise and agree often because the majority rules.

But no one has said that individual rights have decreasing value based on society (the majority) switching its core values. If I choose to remain a moral, Bible-based believer, should I not reject the attempts of a few to call my belief system outdated.

In this great melting pot, we relish definition of opinions and beliefs as additional flavors that support our individualism. On one hand, we seek to unify the melting pot but on the other hand we seek to stand out as individuals. The Bible explains this as not being able to serve two masters; you will hate the one and love the other.

The people of our country (those absent of a belief system and those lukewarm about the one they follow) do not want to separate godly behaviors and standards from secular influences because existing in the same realm with the godly provides credence to ungodliness. I liken it to the Mafia making great monetary commitments to the church. You can't fool God.

So another strategy is to attack. The moral system is filled with uncommitted administrators who panic at the growing wave of dissenters. But dissent is not against individual moral structure. It is dissent against the system perpetuated by a religious, spiritual doctrine that supports the God of the universe. Don't get angry with the Kurt Cameron's of the world because they have read, studied, and followed the belief system that has been handed down by believers for thousands of years. Distinct individuals and groups develop and modify their own systems of right. And the rights and privileges of individuals infuse these systems with a righteous stamp of self-expression; even when it conflicts with the high ideals suggested by an informal standard.

Absent of the ungodly, we cannot recognize godliness. Yes, we need each other and we function better as a team. It is an outgrowth of evil to focus on individual differences because they are personal and will tend to separate people---separation by differences being a primary objective of evil. But even the Bible recommends not associating with evil...come out from among them. But if everyone comes out from among the unrighteous, how will they know the acts of righteousness?

When society labels the wannabe righteous as too judgmental, too self-righteous, and too religious; then society turns on itself and actually obfuscates a potentially helpful body of thought. The labels concerning religious folks (Christians) are repeated until most accept the perspective that everyone should just attend to their own business. But the purpose of the righteous is in effect to educate people on how to care about one another's situation.

American society demands moral flexibility so that individual rights can flourish, or at least be respected enough to be left alone. So, individual rights are put at odds against principled individuals when principled individuals support a stable, but contradictory moral infrastructure. This moral infrastructure is disavowed when it reflects consideration by supporting a standard societal right that involves correction of individual rights for the greater good.

Oddly, a fair-society has unfairly removed God from the moral code, placing the administration and foundation of the code upon the backs of sinful, compromising human beings with loud, powerful voices.

So, flexibility is a must because high moral standards degrade as more people devise excuses and side philosophies to circumvent the righteousness of morality. Consequences for murder degrade by reasoning of why someone did it. Consequences for sexual immorality degrade as more things are taken off the sexually immoral listing. Humanity reshapes its definition of high moral codes absent of God so as not to show favoritism, not to offend; and to evade the guilt that so often accompanies godly disobedience. And if you don't accept the existence of God, you empower your right to not be judged by godly principles; those irritating principles that one should follow just because.

But what if God or a God-led society established the high moral code in complete awareness of humanity's predilection towards falling short; with a safeguard that some prophets would speak with boldness about what God desires contrary to fleshy direction.

God offers stability, and God offers an end to the fleshy searching of self, with a beginning that never ends. With God, you find yourself and the way in which you should interact with life in you and around you. With God, you train and learn from the inside out; thereby spiritually managing the secular environment's impact on your soul.

American Soul

The pages of American history scream with the blood and torment of enslaved African Americans (American Soul or AMS). It appeared to be the pages screaming but it was the black words on the page that screamed. The white pages of the history books increased and for a respite, America served us a cold plate of post-slavery Jim Crow with familial, political, economic, and psychological oppression. And some people said they should appreciate being the included in the book because it was better than being in Africa.

So, says you, says you. Render a hint of the unfairness concerning the oppressive threads of injustice that weave through society and the history books, and watch mysterious agendas unfold against us; and hear shouts vilifying and chastising us as if we rudely and unwarrantedly demanded the right to speak the truth. It reminds me of a game my teenage son would play with me. Upon getting caught doing wrong, he would get angry and raise his voice and storm out of room as if he was dealt an injustice in being caught. My persistent calm would invoke a greater level of wraith and indignation.

Finally, I met his defense with my own indignation at his defense of the indefensible. Upon raising my voice and reminding him of his own guilt, he would finally end the charade.

My son attempted to use his teenage angst and perceptions to override the rules. But the rules had been established to provide order for the system for ongoing conduct and excellence of behavior. Whether he believed in them or not, the rules were not to be broken at his individual caprice. I had the authority. Unfairness is often difficult to perceive or admit by those in authority because order aligns with authority's perception that its authority is working. Disobedience or a claim of unfairness is seen as a cry for correction by authority. My house, my rules.

When the rules are unevenly applied, the authority who administers the rules clearly undermines his or her purpose of having a unified, stable following.

Are you saying unfair because you are getting the lesser of the benefits when your lack of effort may be the cause of your dissatisfaction? Or are you saying unfair because you have a legitimate grievance; and if so, can you prove it?

A standard and just moral code established by the moral standards of generations of intelligent humanity should make this answer the same for all. The caste system undermines the authority of the United States in caring for the concerns of all people. It systematically labels the language of separation and insecurity. Supporters of the caste system think they have merely sentenced social and political fairness to the cracks and crevices of subjectivity. But right is right. The dilemma for the victim of unfairness is that the unfair perpetrator will always use the negative argument that the victim has been treated fairly but wants a handout of undeserved benefits. And the question arises that if the oppressor admits guilt, how long must one pay for the unfair actions and what degree of repentant actions can one consider as enough?

Since the payoff or reparations for such action would change the mixture of the economic pie that is America, let's not deal with it; while AMS faces the economic, political, and social degradation of the lack of positive, objective decision-making.

America's sense of right cannot be trusted by AMS. The country gave reparations to the Jews for WWII's murderous degradation of their people and this country took no action to initiate nor conduct the Holocaust. America gave reparations for the Japanese who were interned in camps during WWII. America gave casinos, land, and tax breaks to Native Americans whose land they stole. To AMS America gave affirmative action programs which were deemed unconstitutional.

Early colonists came to America to escape religious persecution. Yet, the physical and idyllic foundation of this great country of religious refuge was carved out on the backs, will, and soul of

African slaves. The systemic slavery supported by the government, law enforcement, educational and religious organizations (including Sunday School teachers) and societal norms, bred and ingrained seeds of hatred and mistrust as an integral part of this country.

Ralph Ellison in his 1952 novel, The Invisible Man, states: "I am not ashamed of my grandparents for having been slaves. I am only ashamed of myself for having at one time been ashamed."

I was proud to be in a loving household with my great-uncle and –aunt who had adopted me soon after birth; but for a brief period in my childhood, I was ashamed of my father's occupation. He worked at the local phosphate mine---a man's job---but he was the janitor. But I learned that he could not be defined solely as a janitor because he owned several properties next to and around our home. I learned to appreciate him for who he was and what he had accomplished despite the many obstacles in life; including the obstacle of being a black man working and caring for a family in the south.

I watched as my powerful father spoke truth to the neighborhood; and had me deliver fresh fish wrapped in newspaper to various people in the community. I wondered how he determined who got fish from week to week. I watched as he stood up and cocked his rifle after some white racists threw an empty soda can into our boat as we fished in Lake Winterset. I watched as a white gas station attendant in Georgia scolded him like a little boy and turned him around after asking to use the restroom. I reflected on all of these memories and more as I held the door handle to keep him from running outside naked, while he suffered from dementia.

And love poured from my heart because I knew that he was near the end of his life. He had a glazed, watery-look in his eyes and he seemed sorrowful at his own condition. I knew that he could have been so much more because he had accomplished so much with such little education. Mr. Handy, as the neighborhood called him, had left his mark. If only I could accomplish one-third of what he had accomplished, with my greater amount of resources.

He took in three boys who were not his progeny. He treated us and willed property to us as if we were blood. America lost and the community lost; not because people would not invest in him. We lost because the city and the country had it rigged for him to fail.

Ralph Ellison revealed the dichotomous nature of African Americans (American Soul) in seeking to grab a piece of the American Dream while escaping our primarily laborious, slave-ridden, oppressed, deprived past. The book addressed various platforms and conflicting opinions within our community. In 2013, that book, *Invisible Man*, was determined to have "no literary value" for the folks in Randolph County, NC.

A high school girl protested the contents of the book and the school board followed in kind. One girl took offence to the book and she was able to have this great literary work taken off the shelf. Take note that the book, written in 1952, won the 1953 National Book Award for fiction.

The book has been recognized by many critics as being a masterpiece; and reading some of the quotes, one can readily determine it as being a looking glass into the soul of 1950's

American Soul's conflicting culture---hate the oppressor's behavior but love the oppressor and the country. Avoid the shame of oppression, while unassumingly acknowledging the role of the oppressors, while still trying our best to improve our situation. We still love the country that our ancestors helped to build but we question just how much love should we show because we have never been offered the opportunity to grieve.

Yes, grieve. Not to offer some quotas or programs or ceremonies, but to grieve about the horrendous lives of our grandparents and those ancestors who were actually one or two generations from slavery. We grieve for those who felt the whip, the torture, and the torment of another man's dreams causing our dreams to fade, generation by generation. We want mainstream America to know that we have forgiven you but don't take us for granted. Right; it may be a little too late.

Ralph Ellison expressed the social, emotional, and intellectual conflict of the American Soul (AMS) in the twentieth century. He sought to reveal the difficulty in being both black and American. Who would have thought that this would still serve as an area of conflict in 2014?

In the post-Civil War era, the United States was not expending much effort to shake the remnants of slavery and social injustice; and as modern times reveal, the struggles don't just go away. As a matter of fact, the majority was angry with AMS for being different, for not being slaves and competing for more. They mistrusted us because we had a right to be extremely angry; especially as they flaunted their good-life and economic American Dream all in our faces.

The book by the late Mr. Ellison, has great literary value; and it is ridiculously ignorant and apathetic (or pure racist) that some soul on the board could not perceive the book as having value for some people, somewhere. It helps to shed light on the long period of adjustment for a country learning, rather reluctantly, how to incorporate people whom they once enslaved and abused, as a free-functioning aspect of a striving-to-be-unified country.

The Randolph County school board reconsidered the ban in a meeting on September 25, 2013; perhaps due to public outcry. The book has been reinstated.

How is it that conflicting views on extremely powerful and meaningful subjects continue to exist? Is it our cultural differences that make for such confusion? Partially. Our cultures encompass differing family values, viewed through experiential lenses. The main thrust of AMS has been to survive by any means necessary, in America. In the midst of America's capitalistic bloom, a central bulb filled with its human energy force has lived by the antithesis of that bloom. The ever-growing tidal wave of mainstream culture to eliminate pulsating, debilitating proof of the negative ramifications of slavery and Jim Crow in America is actually an attack against our culture. American Soul is filled with ambivalence. We want to feel accepted as Americans instead of keeping watch to ensure that we are not pushed to the outer realm of white America's inner circles. But we also want to be accepted on our own terms, with our own "hybrid" culture.

Hybrid culture isn't a bad phrase but a realistic one. We are not African and the African bloodline can be traced in many cultures. The attribute of having dark skin and our ancestry of being enslaved foreigners bred on this soil enhances our connection to Africans. But modern African immigrants want to distinguish themselves from AMS whose ancestors were enslaved for centuries in America.

In the Bible, the young Rehoboam was 41 years old when he began to reign over Israel. He inherited his rule from his father, the wise King Solomon. In the transition to Rehoboam's rule, the people made specific requests as to changes they desired. The political activist, Jeroboam, led the people to inquire of the king for tax relief since Solomon had taxed the people heavily. The older counsel advised Rehoboam to speak with the people in a civil manner, being fair to comply with the requests of the people. His young advisors told him to be tough and henceforth the words:

> "Whereas my father laid upon you a heavy yoke, so
> shall I add tenfold thereto. Whereas my father chastised you

with whips, so shall I chastise you with scorpions. For my littlest finger is thicker than my father's loins; and your backs, which bent like reeds at my father's touch, shall break like straws at my own touch." (I Kings 12:11).

As a result of such cruelty and insensitive aloofness, the people rebelled and the ten northern tribes formed Israel; leaving Rehoboam king over two southern tribes, Judah and Benjamin (known as Judah).

The tribal issues in the aforementioned situation were political but generational issues as well. Perhaps, age plays just as important a part in our skewed viewpoints of what is fair and unfair in America as experiences in other arenas. This would mean that familial, religious, generational, economic, and cultural views can taint perspectives on what is fair and unfair; and what one group considers fair, may be considered unfair by another group.

Black nationalism was another area of consideration in the time of Ralph Ellison's writing. Rehoboam represented a historical misdeed that has been conducted for centuries in which leaders who had been given much power, chose to abuse the people or a group of people; thinking that the people were purposed to serve them instead of them being answerable to the people. Such flaws in thinking create spiritual leadership gaps where people develop misguided concepts of leadership and direction. Such spiritual gaps cannot be corrected readily by common sense because society has chosen to abide by the flexibility of that which perpetuates these gaps in leadership. People with power created by these gaps often refuse to give it up.

Worst of all, victims and witnesses to the abuse become potential disciples with flawed philosophies that can be perpetuated for generations. And the whole suffers as a result. Soul to pay.

When these philosophies provide a minimum of benefits (especially financial benefits in a capitalistic society) governmental agencies make the mistake of staying with the philosophies until the bitter end. American Soul (AMS) have borne the bitter constraints of slavery and Jim Crow that limited our upward mobility, stifled our education, and restricted our voices, as familial, economic and psychological remnants of slavery hang about our necks.

This treachery against the "one nation" concept of a United

States was masqueraded as a just cause for maintaining or securing the continuation of the white race; and the perpetuation of an America that supported elitism and classism. Some will say: but that was over 150 years ago.

Correction: slavery ended in 1865 and Jim Crow and racial oppression continued strong into the 1960's. Civil Rights legislation tried to make things right going forward, not to correct anything in the past. Affirmative action quotas which tried to give American Soul a foot up was ruled unconstitutional because it discriminated against the rights of Caucasians. The demons of mainstream society sit back when convenient to confirm the insanity of a social, racial disaster; while quietly creating irreconcilable situations with justified laws and strategic inaction.

It was just the other day when a youth filled with potential was tragically hounded by gang members and shot like a dog in the streets. It was like yesterday when the local police mistakenly shot a hail of bullets into another unarmed youth. It is a daily possibility for some talk show radio host to proclaim that black folks are the cause of America's woes when that's all that has been placed on American Soul---woe.

Gangs in a country with the strongest military force in the world? Hate-mongers on the governmentally-monitored airwaves? Although the voices have been reduced in number and we have continued to make progress, the voices of racists, greedy radio hosts and selfish, inconsiderate, unsympathetic politicians speak a more concealed but painfully similar message. They create issues where none exists by berating AMS as if to follow a young Rehoboam's lead: *tax (berate, terminate, chastise, oppress) them more because that's how we will keep them obedient. The mainstream appears to feel as if they make* one slip-up it will initiate a continuous run of AMS presidents, media personalities, black

CEO's and television shows.

How does the AMS suffer with so many equal rights, luxuries and opportunities? Should not time have erased the pain, while slowly taking demagogues of racism gently into the night?

Perhaps that is how it should be. But the residue of slavery and economic inequality is so pervasive and deeply entrenched in the seams and layers of society that its unfolding, be it arbitrary or contrived, smothers and irritates like several thick, wool blankets in the spring. The purpose is to keep you warm and it works in the winter but blankets are especially reserved and placed solely on one group of people in the summer and spring. With reason, we toss the hot blankets aside only to face the natural heat of the day...the economy or the same tough issues all Americans face.

Here's a blanket of welfare, incarceration, and a blanket of drugs and violence. But then AMS takes a nap only to wake up with those same hot blankets tossed upon us in the summer and spring. By nature, it was too hot to sleep. We awaken in the middle of the night sweating, and try to kick off the blankets in frustration and restless anger. They want you to forget how long you have borne the burden of the blankets even though it was just last night, and when it becomes a nuisance, they want you to forget who put it on you. Who put this on me; it makes no sense? It's just your former oppressor making sure that you are covered properly.

People were bred, women and children abused, and men emasculated for generations to supply a free labor force for the United States of America. Family life for AMS was and has been an aftermath. Our familial purpose transitioned from perpetuating a labor supply to just surviving by any means necessary. Work and education have not necessarily changed our status because we still have to seek labor (for the most part) among the former oppressor's environment; and we are not always welcome because we are different; and we have shown the resilience of making it to places in society where the doors had to be pushed open.

The United States of America is the celebration of freedom that stole Native American land and enslaved AMS to sow and harvest the produce that covered the capitalistic table for the festive United States culture. AMS are the very determined who refused to leave the celebration; despite the dissuasion of the host. We have too much invested.

We are done with slavery but it has continued to have its way with us. It is with awestruck enlightenment that we love family and families. Having seen families torn apart and expecting their families to endure such things year after year, for centuries, our people had to either love regardless of expectations or they learned to never show deep, real emotions for the dread of lost love is often unbearable.

Understand the cultural limitations imposed upon us with the most fundamental, sustaining emotion of all time. Jesus stated the greatest commandment is that we love one another. You could open your heart and love deeply knowing that the earthly master could sell the object of your affections. You could choose to never allow yourself to know deep love and be prepared for disaster; and it may have never come.

Another option (perhaps the most common) would be to develop a hard edge that allows you to function daily without going crazy. That hard edge, in some ways, incorporates your own version of insanity because deep inside your soul, you know that there is a better way. It is the AMS version of PTSD (Posttraumatic Stress Syndrome). Generation after generation, our families pay for the oppressed version of love; the cruel bastardization of love when the slave-master gave only one member of a slave family a chance to live free or to speak like a man while others continued to work in the fields.

That skewed version in which someone cares for you in order to get more out of you. It sounds like a country...and a plantation. It is PTSD because it has psychological ramifications upon AMS as we interact under the auspices of law enforcement, governments, and social mores which branded us as enemies. These conflicts still confront us today.

It is a cruel demonic antithesis of love when oppression provides the covering for a household where kindness and gentleness is offered to selected individuals who have done the master's bidding. Some of the oppressors deceived themselves into thinking that love could be offered and accepted under forceful dictates as long as it was legal.

Look at the animals in the cage closely. "Lillie, I loved you like a daughter and you tried to escape. How dare you hurt me so!" For modern times: "I gave you a job...I let you play basketball and football...I let you make millions, and you still say we're not fair. You still want reparations?"

Today we still see the favor cast upon fair-skinned AMS over those of a darker hue. The historical obstacles are in place where we actually waste time decoding and deciphering love (because we have endured so many faux versions of it) when we are supposed to spend time loving. But some still experience real love and those who manage to grab a piece of it or smell the wondrous scent of it, are among a select view who know that true love does exist. But the few are not enough to combat the erroneous, faux versions of love that dominate a formerly enslaved people who have never had a transitory vehicle to redefine specific understandings of trust, love, friendship, and companionship.

Flawed thinking seeps through and rests in the core of the culture---the women. The PTSD impacts not all, but so many. The ones who have been assigned the roles of soft, gentle, loving, forgiving, and understanding role models. They rock the cradle of AMS and the children often receive misguided messages of how love is supposed to be displayed and pursued because the message was always delivered under an umbrella of deceit.

Unlike a real battlefield, the children suffer with little or no hope of leaving. Generation after generation, born and raised with the expectation of winning the battle within the parameters of the war. The CDC calls it hood disease---as in AMS neighborhood disease--- and reported on May 14, 2014 that 30% of our youth suffer from its effects (according to the Medical Blog). Unfortunately, the youth become adults with PTSD.

The transition from youthful teenager to young adult has been blurred as college and other successful ventures never guaranteed progressive career movements away from trained, habitual, degenerative ideologies. Athletes, movie stars, and other professions that symbolize 'having made it' often fail to pull the young adult male away from the tentacles of the hood. Spiritual warfare becomes evident as so many people question the reasoning of returning to the values that shaped the man.

The values shaped the man along with the environment. The mother who had numerous babies out of wedlock while annually hooked on drugs and men, was still 'mom'. The friends who dealt drugs with no father figure and did everything they could do to survive, were still friends trying to survive. And the dangerous places where they almost didn't make it (which was everywhere) still served as reminders of God's grace and a strong person's unique ability to survive.

When momma and them went to church and sang, "Somehow I made it, through it all God brought me through..." they testified as to the reality of God and everybody got happy because improvement didn't have to occur.

Some youth and adults exhibited the practicality of emotions...being highly perfunctory about the vitals of a mundane existence; getting lost in routine. Church, drugs, stealing, killing, and conning all become routines. Even celebrations become intense with preparation. Everything must be right, whatever right is supposed to be. And there must be food, high in calories with a history of being prepared 'back in the day.' The message is that love requires physical work and must produce meaningful outcomes; and it must be shown despite living conditions.

The ancestors of AMS learned that if you never deeply love, you risk less: and you may be able to get more out of it. You can protect your heart and avoid the pain of an unfulfilled relationship; at the cost of never knowing the benefits of real love. But some took the leap of faith. They trusted when it looked as if their personal needs would not be met. They trusted God and love when it looked as if a better financial decision could be made. They decided to dive headfirst into it despite seeing so many broken-hearts.

And even today, only a few reap the benefits because it is the revelation of such love that can change one's outlook on life and increase one's perseverance in all things. The love of God and the true sacrificial love found in a marriage safely guides the mind and heart towards a spiritual and secular union to which nothing can compare.

We enjoy ourselves when we have someone else to confirm that we are having a good time. And even if we spend time to ourselves, we want others to know that we got away with it and for its brief timeframe, we enjoyed it. Yes, we are all connected. As Rachel Carson enlightens humanity in her book, *"Silent Spring;"* all living things are connected. It's commonsense to know that I can politicize issues at the expense of demoralizing the most downtrodden and poverty-stricken of social classes but it will eventually affect me and my social class.

A country exists as a result of various external forces exerted upon a geologically, homogenous group of people who realize the collective and individual benefits of a common defense, educational, legal, traffic infrastructure, and tax system. Yet, in the midst of it all, one group of miscreants can disavow and cause disillusion among another group of people; thereby ruining the sanctity of thought of one people, one nation.

Eventually, what goes around comes around. We cannot ignore, and neither should we want to ignore, the former oppressor's religion, politics, societal and cultural mores, and desires. After all, we adopted them as our own albeit through the dark lens of slavery, second-class citizenry, and Jim Crow. How easily the former victim perceives the connection and benefits of a united country in which we share fundamental beliefs; as citizens with common goals. We are not suffering from Stockholm Syndrome (we may have been but now its good old commonsense) but our suffering has enabled higher order spiritual and secular thinking. The descendants of slaves have applied spiritual beliefs to real world suffering and to more personal situations and circumstances for hundreds of years.

Yes, we shout and dance about God and godly possibilities because we saw Him in action, housed in our hopes and dreams. In post-Civil War America, we felt our hopes and dreams dashed against the stones as white America hated to see any AMS succeed.

Resilient is defined as, "capable of withstanding shock without permanent deformation or rupture." (Free Merriam-Webster

Dictionary). Since I was a child sitting at the feet of my mother and father, listening to their comments as they watched the news on the black-and-white television set, I understood the meaning of resilient. Neither of the two finished middle school and both had established roles within the American Soul (AMS) community and church. This is probably the most difficult concept for other races to understand (other than members of the Jewish faith). We are truly a culmination of constant overcome: black comedians were a blessing despite their profanity. AMS singers and athletes were testimonies not of the goodness of the United States but as to our resilience. AMS rappers with their profanity and excessive use of the N-word, and derogatory comments about women, still reflect economic empowerment beyond our downtrodden past.

Just as the lessons we learned living next to the drug-dealer and adulterers who all went to the same church, we value the spirit of overcome to the point of by any means necessary. The "thugged-out", drug-dealing, ongoing murders of AMS youth is not my culture. Welfare and fear of cops is not my culture. Waiting for the next crime to be committed near me or upon my family is not my culture. Thinking about not being promoted or not applying for a job because of racism isn't how I want to think. These aforementioned things are forced upon the AMS mindset but we don't have to accept them. Every positive action I take in the face of discrimination prompts me to work harder and to be more diligent; and to remember that overcome is an attribute of my people who have been called out by God.

Our meetings, celebrations, and barbecues were challenges to the powers that be that we would not live sadly among the shadows of life simply because mainstream society sought to regulate us to such dominions. Our personal relationships became empowering vehicles that confirmed we were not in this battle alone. Our religion, called liberation theology, simply attested to our suffering like Jesus Christ and that one day, we too, would overcome the trials of this world.; while still yet in the land of the living.

Yes, resilient is a wonderful word to describe the progeny of former slaves in America. Constantly seeking definition and a name other than the ones that a history of oppression has given us, we search among names given for a unique, hybrid-sorts of people. We are of African ancestry but we are not Africans who become US citizens, or African Americans. We are American Soul, forged from the most hopeless of times, in which we learned to persevere with hope and a godly spirit. We emerged from the deepest, darkest despair of the United States, despite the thuggish American behavior that brought us here, leaving behind the African continent, where time itself began.

God allowed inhumane, horrific, brutality to correct, and heal and shape a people, on a timeline only known to him. These one-time conquerors were conquered and brought to America---the land of the free and the home of the brave. AMS surnamed, "the resilient ones," who have borne the indignities of the country; worked to fulfill a dream that encompassed the most basic of human rights; while simultaneously being served the antithesis of those rights.

The vastness of slavery's sickening shadow cannot be fully observed through any one lens. It was and it is a social issue. It was a physical brutality that carries deep wounds and a scarlet shame; and some anger. It was and is a psychological reinforcement of dominance which perpetuated frustration and lowered expectations. It was a familial issue that mutated our emotional responses and skewed the lines of authority within families; with long-lasting effects.

It was America's choice for American Soul to bear a continual burden that would change the representative face of slavery from the Hebrews to a much darker hue. Unique and unequally oppressive, American slavery is referenced as the cruel, brutal, and barbaric conquest of a people's culture and dignity. Yes, the people were freed; yes, times changed; yes, we became true American Soul, but we were never issued anything substantive for having our future (children, mothers, fathers, and mores) convoluted and infected in a trade for the future of a capitalistic master plan. The mortgaging of the United States written on the backs of AMS and signed with our ancestors blood. We are the resilient progeny of godly resiliency. We may have ancestral PTSD but we don't suffer from it; not like the children.

A time comes when memories of atrocities fade and become fairy-tale-like stories of bygone days. So, once-upon-a-time, children of slavery's children's, children's, children's, children, can't understand the angst of being sold like cattle; and tortured like terrorists; and for good measure legally being given a freedom that regulated these same people to second-class citizenry. And the fear of us was so great that every time it looked as if we had a representative among our people 'escaping' they would conspire against him or her, and grab the threat by the neck and hang him or toss him backwards, or kill him and burn his legacy.

Time heals most wounds and after a little while, the stories become the folklore of legends. Grandfather, like his father before him, actually risked his life and stood on the porch with a cocked shotgun in his hands. He boldly told the white man to never touch his children again as long as he lived; and he knew the man would return with some hooded friends and wreak havoc on his family. So, he took everything and everybody and headed to Minnesota and changed the family name to something he liked. This led to one last change: the Dacosta family, which should have been initially called the Yoruba family, became the Freemans.

They learned that you can't have everything in life and the tradeoff for peace was something to rejoice. Yes, the subtle societal harassments continued and scarred us almost just as much as the lynching. Allow white folks to have the sidewalk; never look a white person in the eye. When a crime is committed against you by a white person, you will be found guilty so don't call the police and don't go to trial. Get an education but your jobs will still be menial because businesses reserve good jobs for Caucasians. Restrooms and water fountains and riding the bus all carry racial scarring. AMS pay your taxes but you will have old, used textbooks that the white folks no longer want or need. Pay your taxes but black-on-black crime will be accepted. And American society still continues to pay for our distrust of local, state, and federal governments and law enforcement agencies.

Such actions taught us that it was acceptable, beneficial, and often necessary to start over. Society would make a place for us but we could never plan for it; it was too unpredictable. It was the impromptu kindness of the slave master after he had sold your children. Day by day, Lord. We didn't expect much but then came a generation (it had to happen) expecting the same rights and privileges of other American citizens. Start-overs often offend people set in their ways; and some distrust arises as we attempt to coax older generations into delving into the new confidence of corrected mores.

We adapted culturally, emotionally, socially, and independently; without a guide book on how to do it. Stay away from them and don't remember your history because it was filled with trash anyway. Slavery compromised your real history as descendants of kings and queens.

The right to participate in capitalism is a right and with a good education, a citizen can take maximum advantage of that right. The American slave-ridden, guidance for the AMS perspective says it is acceptable to devalue education since physical labor has always been prioritized ahead of academics, for most of us. And a good education still means that you have to get hired by white folks although that is changing.

And even if you can get a good job among people who don't trust you--because they have knowledge of the poor treatment of your people---you have to weigh the benefits of employment verses the psychological trauma of an unpleasant working environment. Should I assimilate and join them as if I am one of them? Or should I remain separate so as not to offend them and not to betray my culture? Capitalism bears the signature of rebellion and innovation; truly attributes identifiable to the descendants of former slaves. Everything that has happened directs us to lukewarm behavior and that does not fly in a capitalistic environment.

We have arrived. In hindsight, society can see how it would have served society best to simply offer fair and humane treatment instead of integration. But continued segregation would have deepened the void of misunderstandings and disassociation with people of color; and new freedoms would have allowed us to perceive the depth of physical, social, and psychological traumas launched against us.

Hard-working individuals of all races proclaim the fact that it is best to pull yourselves up by your own bootstraps; but the playing field in which I set my feet for balance must be even. James Brown said that he didn't want anyone to give him anything; just open the doors and he would get it himself.

The doors of equality were merely cracked and AMS was allowed to put a few chairs and tables outside the suites until we created separate substandard chamber rooms; with the real freedoms still beyond another door. Sporadically, someone would come to the cracked door and escort one or two AMS inside.

If some effort had been made for correcting the injurious past horrors committed against African-American Souls (reparations); then, and only then, would the AMS race of people shoulder total responsibility for pulling ourselves up. This move alone would open the floodgates to economic empowerment and capitalism for all citizens. Of course, this would also make AMS less dependent on the majority race and it would have increased land ownership and financial viability among us. The fearful would see the threat to white supremacy and take violent and political action.

As in any relationship in which a subordinate wants out, providing economic support increases the potential for success by the subordinate. As long as the subordinate struggles, it is a confirmation that the supervisor/oppressor to subordinate relationship should not change.

Sadly, it is still considered good politics by certain parties to disparage the AMS as if such maneuvering will get candidates elected in 2013. These political powers have party agendas against a group of people who have been attacked since forcefully being brought to this country in chains...and the fact that politicians can get elected and reelected based on their racists and discriminatory stances of what these people don't deserve is a byproduct of slavery. Good politics in the 2012 Presidential election still entails keeping laws from being passed that would benefit minorities; and hiding important viewpoints among the folderol of inconsequential, irrelevant, or zero-priority-issues.

For the debacle that has been called governance, no one should get reelected on the Republican side and very few on the Democratic side. The country needs to show the government that we shall not be subjected to continuing lack while the politicians have plenty and get stalemated in personal agendas and vendettas.

Good politics in 2012 involved repealing laws that minorities no longer need because they discriminate against good white folks. Good Republican politics, in 2012, emphasized, almost heartlessly, smaller government despite the help needed by the disenfranchised and the supervision needed by the capitalist entrusted with fueling our economy. The Tea Party proclaims a foundation of thought and righteousness by combining the words, "God and Country"; then ruthlessly stands against compromise and reconciliation as if their perspective is errorless, and without the needed support of the democracy. The country pays a heavy price for having demagogues in high places.

The Republican brand, with which I have shared some perspectives in the past, now takes the least of minority issues and conjures up discriminatory concerns supported by Republican pundits. Conservative talk-radio stirs up the masses and reinforces inconsiderate and racist agendas that have become a bastion for developing slick racist dialect. The former Klansman has turned in his white, pointed-hood robes for business suits and stimulating conversation that hints at racist ideologies. He has hunkered down and refused to assimilate into the melting pot that would be the American Dream.

The revolution wasn't televised but you know it when you see it, and more is to come. Yes, more souls have to pay. Those "devoid of a soul" (stated in a December 31, 2012 Huffington Post article by Luke Johnson, as stated by Republican Jon Huntsman about his own party), will still have to pay with the agony and despair of God's consequences for abusing innocent souls.

We have learned, revolution comes to those who demand change. The "Occupy" movement has shown us a sampling of what needs to be done but the financially equipped AMS have a greater advantage. They don't have to finance the movement but they can commit to the greatest involvement for the people. Professional athletes, financial wizards/business owners, and AMS leaders can lead the march on Wall Street for internships; for colleges for more accessible grants; and for cooperative administrations and their support of the aforementioned jobs.

The greatest question involves the future concepts of country to be held by our children. Mainstream society devalued education for AMS and then tried to reverse the trend; and this has created quite a quagmire for us. When the people revolt, what will they understand about the revolution and how will they fulfill our end of the bargain which is to prop up mainstream society for the enduring status and well-being of this great country? The hybrid creation of America engulfs all souls until everyone seeks to find a happy middle where we can share a common purpose. There is no such place. Drastic change eradicates political talk that subversively seeks to stall change. Drastic action by all souls changes things and those with old-fashioned ideologies change or get left behind in the area of socialization, politics, and sometimes economics.

But some say---those who want to make slavery fairytales--- forget about slavery because it did have some benefits; after all, your people are in the greatest country in the world. And I say, "What was the price? It was too high; and someone has to pay down the moral and social stigma of the deficit."

The John Locke Foundation allowed a freelance blogger named Tara Servatius (who posted a picture of President Obama chained while wearing high heels and standing over a bucket of brand-name chicken) to resign. The picture was posted on Monday, March 19, 2012, and she resigned on Thursday. In doing this I must say that the foundation genuinely touched my heart and caused me to pause for a minute. This is a young country and mistakes are constantly being made; but somehow, somewhere, some people seem to get it. They can disagree and remain civil and expect civil behavior from others. Rick Henderson, managing editor of the foundation's journal, issued a statement decrying such a lack of civility. I salute you Rick Henderson and the John Locke Foundation.

The author Rachel Carson's book Silent Spring is credited with starting the environmental movement and bringing to the world's attention the fact that we are all connected; and what one does impacts others. Yet, we can't seem to understand that this references civil rights, politics, religious intolerance, media-driven philosophies; and everything else on the planet done in large numbers with passionate commitments. Yes, we have individual rights but large groups of people and their decisions will impact the world. We are all connected, and there's a price to pay for every ill-conceived thought that manifests into action that does not align with the spirit of humanity and righteousness.

Unfortunately, Jonathan Ferrell paid the ultimate price and in large part, due to perceptions conjured up by mainstream society. He played football for FAMU in 2009 and 2010. He had moved to Charlotte, NC from Tallahassee, Florida. On the night of September 15, 2013, Jonathan had crashed his car. Apparently, it was a serious enough crash that he had to exit the vehicle by knocking out the rear window. Mr. Ferrell's blessings were great in that he did not get severely injured in the accident but he still had to seek help among America's most dangerous element for AMS: the southerner, in particular, the southern police officer.

He ran to the nearest household and began knocking on the door. It was about 2:30 in the morning. A lady, thinking him to be a burglar, called 911. What burglars knock on the door, I don't know of any. Now the call is out for a burglar when it should have been out for a man who was seeking help after suffering a car crash. I can imagine that media perceptions and every racist thought since birth, flowed through the homeowner's mind.

Here comes the police officer; surely, he will sort things out and provide assistance. Officer Kerrick observed a black man, Jonathan Ferrell running towards him. He did not think that a citizen could have been running towards him seeking assistance. Did he yell halt or I'll shoot? Did he at least warn the young man that a report was out on a burglar?

The police officer shot the innocent American citizen seeking help and the shooting personifies how mainstream America's perception of AMS continues to get us killed.

The Moral Code

There is a common moral code that resides within each of us; no matter how we behave (perhaps social deviants excluded). God has instilled within our DNA, a value system that screams killing, sexual debauchery, stealing, and abuse of our bodies, is wrong. Committed fornicators found in the heterosexual and homosexual ranks have to feel the tug of conscience as they indulge in acts that rebel against the God inside of them. As time passes, the environment in which we grow either enhances and nurtures the code or we learn new pathways to avoid adhering to the code.

The family provides the first line of defense in administering the code properly. Two parent households increase the chance of proper moral code administration although one parent may be lacking in communication skills. Nevertheless, the more messengers the greater the chance of getting more messages accepted by the family members. This still does not negate the fact that a person with the right message can practice actions that contradict the proper moral message until the improper message becomes ingrained in the soul.

At the core of many families was religion. When highly moralistic reasoning souls abandoned the commitment to organized religion, the inherent message that God was supporting the moral commitment was no longer stated, implied, or inferred.

Why should the child do the right thing if no one is watching all the time? As a matter of fact, the child progressing through various stages of maturity will test the consequences of improper actions; even with religion. In a home with an inconsistent or nonexistent moral message, this testing will occur while failing to see negative consequences, and he or she may conclude that immorality can be fun and worth the risk.

Instead of supporting the moral code which sustains civic stability, and social order provided by religion, society debates the authenticity of religion and which one is the best. Most religions teach morality in foundational principles, so, the end of religion in school settings brought about by political-correctness, also brought about the demise of a reinforcement tool for family values and the moralistic training inherent in religions. This reinforcement tool happens to also exist as a foundational principle in most societies.

Friends and acquaintances reinforce or develop messages within the individuals. They pick-up where the family left off; or they fill the gaps that the family failed to address. Each person outside of the family brings his or her own moral code. Our parents would say be careful of the company you keep.

Today, as a society, we begin to see the results. Children lie with no conscience. They will look you in the face and even cry when they want to convince you that they are telling the truth. They have no problem with starting a physical confrontation, retaliating after delivering the first blow, and having a prepared lie that addresses their self-defense. Other children gather around and eagerly open their mouths in support of the initiator; they lie without being asked, and it is morally reprehensible. They have seen the consequences of improper behavior on the Internet, and it seems as if every notable, confrontational act of disobedience gets the most number of "likes," or followers.

Another immoral result is rapidly increasing. A middle-aged man decided that he didn't want to go to work at his job on a particular day. He staged a break-in of his home; leaving the windows open and telling 911 that he came home and found his front door and windows wide open. He also told the police that his television was on the floor and he did not put it there. The police asked if he saw a vehicle leaving the area when he arrived home. He stated that he did and he continued the lie by giving a description of this imaginary vehicle that left as he was pulling up to his house. He did all of this contrary to his wife's more logical opinion not to engage the law with his devious desires to stay home from work.

The man did not know it was against the law to do what he did...filing a false police report. But he should have weighed the moral impropriety, his wife's counsel, and the valuable time of law enforcement prior to making such a selfish decision.

In another situation, a teenage couple did not have a place to have sex so they engaged in the act in a hotel lobby. Upon being asked to leave, the male turned belligerent and pushed the female employee against the wall while complaining about his dilemma. They then turned and ran out of the hotel.

A lack of moral fiber leads to leaks in small amounts, in small places, until the leaks grow. Most will get used to the leaks and wonder if anyone---any one person---will ever stop them.

Society provides the last stand for moral code reinforcement and it reveals consequences for not following the code. The good thing about society is that its consequences are supposed to be universal and what it establishes, everyone must follow. As long as it is fair across the board, society can stabilize governments and assure people that those who do wrong will be punished; and provide an additional reasoning as to why we should follow the rules.

But the soul of the country pays when the basic moral code of society is applied and enforced unevenly. The soul of the country pays when everyone can identify a segment of society that has more than its share of problems and society itself bears some responsibility for these problems. The soul of the country pays when citizens can identify segments of society which don't bear the problems as much as others.

Children have learned to lie with no fear of consequences so an embattled pair will lie to the point of having witnesses testify; and they will still lie. AMS learned that people could smile in your face and still consider you as the n-word. We learned that unfairness, dishonesty, mistrust, condemnation, and imprisonment, accompanied our lives along with our ethnicity in America. We shared the stories of an unevenly administered moral code that sent AMS to war in Viet-Nam while the children of the former oppressors paid not to go to war; or went to college. We shared stories of hard-working people losing their primary bread-winner after being snatched in the night by hooded, cowardly night-riders. We shared the witnessing of white folks and white governments snatching land from hard-working AMS. We shared the testimony of victory against all odds; despite the low-economic class, the favoritism offered white colleagues, and the racist environs.

Our moral code knew of the God who delivers and that was reinforced after 254 years of slavery. But we had to make adjustments to American society's moral code that was trod upon by the very society that advocated it. We made adjustments to society's viewpoint of the drug-dealer, prostitutes, gamblers, and con men who resided next door in our communities. We regarded the bankers, principals, teachers, and legitimate business owners with great respect. They all were trying to survive against the odds while quietly rebelling against the society which most of us wanted to be a part. Our conflicting hearts pushed a the foot on our necks.

Religion stabilized our communities against hatred and self-deprecation. The God who freed us and united us in the cotton fields was still the God of our hope. We accepted the sinners and saints as one community against the injustice placed upon us by society.

America suffered for disavowing the contributions of AMS and designing pogroms against us. As a result of it happening, the memory of a false moral code cannot be erased...we shall never forget. The old moral code was not one established by God but one agreed upon by a greedy, devious society who filled it with exceptions. America suffers and AMS suffers more. We should have been given the land, the money, or the time, to grieve, to heal wounds, and to assess the impact of conflicting, separate moral standards designed to maintain an American caste system.

As a child, I saw a double-standard of senseless oppression and I heard my mother and father speak with sadness regarding oppressive acts. No one had to tell me that America did not treat black folks fairly. I simply wondered why we didn't shoot the men who threw the beer can in our boat; after all, dad had the rifle cocked and they deserved it. I wondered why my tough father didn't turn around and slap the Caucasian gas attendant in the face and use the restroom anyway.

It is the concept that AMS youth today don't understand. They Speak boldly of the actions they would have taken had they faced the injustices wrought by the caste. I tell them how tough my father was and what he endured for the family instead of getting killed. They say that slavery took place over 200 years ago, so why do we need to worry about this now? They live in AMS regions, filled with black folks and communities with black businesses.

I tell them that injustices against AMS were justified by the law; starting with the local police who usually assumed the guilt of the black person despite the facts. If the situation moved beyond the local law enforcement level, the judicial system, including federal law, often projected a monstrous obstacle that appeared insurmountable. All of this occurred among people who had been enslaved, denied education and equal opportunities; and who had very little signs for hope.

It really is a slap in the face to reflect upon the good 'ole days when those times were made good for white folks on the backs of second-class citizenry for blacks. The possibilities have always been unlimited but the white elephant in the room keeps getting ignored. Without oppression, without discrimination; AMS would fairly govern an increasingly moral, fair-minded society.

Well, we can feel free to reflect upon such possibilities considering the lack of respect and consideration given to a down-trodden group of people. It is our right to speculate that unbiased, fair-minded leadership would be better and fairer for the country; and the sooner the better.

Why is it that specific people would make great potential leaders for a country that has maintained a powerful status in the world with a preponderance of biased white, male leaders? The answer to this comes in the form of perseverance and resiliency. AMS survived centuries of lack, disrespect, and oppression. My eyes were opened to the needs of family and other people with the application of my religion's principles, after being emotionally oppressed. After talking with many people, I have noticed that we who have suffered and come to the enlightened understanding of others, have attained a unique perspective that experience alone cannot supply.

AMS can relate to economic downturns, family needs, governmental intervention, law enforcement, and civil disobedience.

Members of Congress need to get used to the idea of a person of color in high government positions so the next time an AMS gets elected President there won't be so much turbulence created just to ensure that he doesn't get credited with a job well-done. We---all American citizens---paid for the reaction of Congress to an AMS president with six years of governmental ineptitude and racist maneuvering.

What I love about such predicaments is the obvious political cover provided by the racist agenda of party-goers. Did they create such tremendous roadblocks to political reform due to the President's color or his political party's ideologies? We know but only a few will own up to the racist conversations that proceeded the racist emails and other media stories.

The moral code established by society has to has some authenticity with it; it has to be evenly applied and believed on by the majority of people and participating minorities. The majority can relay coded morality by means of institutions; including the justice system and corporations. Why does this great buy-in need to occur. If the moral code is deemed unfair or unevenly applied, the minority of people will point out how it is unfair and will revolt against the moral code even when it makes sense to follow it.

And eventually, this leads to systemic destruction. We have seen this in the form of various institutions: marriage and child-birth which affected child-rearing, which affected children's education. Much of what is transpiring today is a result of unfair moral code application. The socio-economic system wasn't fair and this led to more of AMS being incarcerated because the justice system supported the socio-economic verdict upon us. Our ancestors recorded the unfairness and the injustices and we knew not to trust the system that developed the moral guidelines by which we were to live.

If you don't trust the moral guidelines, you don't follow the rules; and you still expect little consequences because others are getting away with it. The school system is filled with these kinds of children: children who don't really expect to face the consequences of wrong-doing. Most of us from past generations marvel at this phenomenon because we grew up facing consequences and suffering that were not due to our own actions. Flip the script and find that now our younger generation expect to get away with things that they should face severe consequences; and due to the uneven application of justice...they do.

For solutions to adjust our moral thinking one has to only look as far as religion. Despite the dirty behavior of some pastors and religious people, we need to remain determined and faithful that we are moral people ordained by God to live holy lives. We remain steadfast and immovable in our spiritual thinking and actions due to our faithful attempts to emulate Jesus Christ.

Now in the past, we could be fairly loose with this emulation. Christians do wrong things that other sinners do but we don't claim it, we want to get rid of it (most of the time). This looseness towards God's word has been manifested in the place where the message is loud and clear: the music.

Music for AMS has been socially and economically empowering. When enslaved we sang code words for escape and to tell the master openly how we felt: "Every body talkin' 'bout heaven ain't goin' to heaven, heaven." While continuously being treated unfairly, we sang about love. When the drug craze captured our attention we sang about feeling good. And when it was time to demand our rights we sang, "Say it loud. I'm Black and I'm Proud!" Thanks James Brown.

Music has been an influential part in motivating and inspiring our culture. Thanks Chuck D. But what in the world does our music do now?

Rap Music and rappers are not responsible for our low moral standards. After all, people accept music as some defining addition or enhancement to their current position in life; a little more than simply entertainment. There are timeless songs which invoke strength and spiritual encouragement without being labeled as Christian or spiritual music. But we are a culmination of lenses, including familial, social, cultural, communal, and parental. Our ongoing change is affected by what we allow to enter our souls. Music provides great support for spiritual and therefore progressive change because it tends to be semi-ubiquitous and in hearing it, we know that someone somewhere agrees with our reasons to think and act the way we do.

So, what happens when the airwaves are filled with vitriolic, misogynistic, powerful rhythmic beats? Some music is predominated by entrepreneurial thugs whose braggadocios chants inspire others to compete; or confirm that a street past of thuggish behavior can lead to millions.

When we examine the content of the lyrics and our past, today's airwaves are filled with rap lyrics that are self-deprecating vehicles of dismay. Our young people saw the American Dream and decided to write about the obstacles in their way, while achieving it. It was a brilliant stroke that most would have thought would fail. But the frustration of generations watching the limitations offered to their families while specific groups seemed to have what they wanted was indeed too much.

The production for some of these pieces is brilliant. A 'wall of sound' composed of dynamic highs of rebellious, defiant, strong, and revolutionary imagery is often presented far before hearing the words. Then they talk about women, calling them female dogs and whores (hoes). Then, younger children than the artists start using the words and we ingrain respect issues for each other. The offensive rap lyrics or other music lyrics did not develop the respect issues; the lyrics support these issues.

The self-respect issues came about as we struggled and observed; as we were emotionally tormented and rebelled with horrific consequences; as we screamed and stomped; and went to church. Some

Somewhere along the line, an evenly applied moral code would have merely slowed the slant of profanity-laced music. Rebellion has always made money in America and some ethnic groups have always paid a higher price than others.

Other cultures don't have the tribulations that we have borne as second-class citizenry combined with the ingenuity and injustice administered. Yet, someone could have said (if they gave a darn) let's not produce such offensive music that will blast throughout communities and out of windows as people drive. Let's go back to making music about love and civil disobedience without thuggish behavior being glorified. Perhaps the music would have still found its way to the forefront of our lives but it would have taken longer. Perhaps the music would have found its way but maybe we would have been able to administer our own moral code to reduce the spiritual wear-and-tear.

The music that we denigrate today is the culminating force of "souls paying" for the prolonged injustices perpetuated by United States citizens against fellow citizens. When you cut yourself and develop a sore (slavery) but that sore's oozing sustains your life; you let the sore ooze. But you never gave a thought to healing the sore as soon as possible and ensuring that a scab grew over it. No, America picked and that sore, and picked at it and ensured that it oozed; even just a little.

Civil and Social Injustice

As Union soldiers advanced through the south, the freed slaves who left the plantation life and followed Union General William Tecumseh Sherman were granted farmland on January 16, 1865, under Special Field Order 15. The civil war was winding down and they were freed, and the heart of a small group in this country felt the need to award these former slaves for the injustices suffered and persevered. Legal terminology would consider that as precedent. The order granted the freed slaves approximately 400,000 acres of confiscated land that stretched from Charleston, South Carolina, to the St. Johns River in Florida. The land grant also included Georgia's sea-islands and the mainland thirty miles from the coast. The land was divided into 40 acre-parcels, among 18,000 freed slave families and blacks living in the area. Some families were also supplied with a mule for plowing. Forty acres and a mule were respectable considerations for a good start to farming. In the fall of 1865, after the war ended, President Andrew Johnson rescinded the order and returned the lands to the original owners. The orders represent knowledge by the United States that reparations were needed and fair, but for some reason, fairness for African Americans has been difficult to attain. Yet, this awareness dwindled into a callous feigned generosity of handouts and special programs (affirmative action) that merely provided a reference point for the continued injustices perpetuated against African Americans. Yes, affirmative action has been ruled unconstitutional; but it was also unconstitutional to disavow reparations after precedence had been established and a debt was established that needed to be paid.

Sharecropping was an agreement or contract between a landlord and a former slave (later the slaves' descendants) in which the oppressed worker as the tenant paid a fraction of the crop to the landlord in exchange for the right to make some economic gain from the landlord's plot of land. The idea of sharecropping should have provided great benefits but as in most contracts, both parties needed to accept and honor mutual benefits. The white owners would create exorbitant expenses (high prices for food and the use of tools) to lessen the economic gain of blacks and ensure the system provided as close to the same benefits as slavery (high profits, low black social status). Former slaves had little recourse---being among four million newly freed persons, having been refused education and given no money to start a new life.

The sharecropper system was so oppressive that blacks would go to the owner to get their share of profits from harvesting the crops and the owner would tell them that they owed him money, having paid out more for exorbitant food and tool usage than they received for the crops. The movie, "Lee Daniels' The Butler" provides further enlightenment on the position of AMS during sharecropping. Many people thought that the scene where Eugene Allen's mother gets raped and his father was shot in the head, was during slavery. But Eugene Allen lived until 2010 and he would have been close to 150 years of age if he had been born when slavery ended.

It's difficult for people to imagine that legal slavery ended but white folks still felt comfortable in hurting and abusing black folks.

Sharecropping ensured that blacks remained poor and without opportunities. The message of devaluing education was still communicated to African Americans as school systems would allow black children time out of school during separate sessions for planting crops and for harvesting them. The former slaves wanted land ownership and the oppressors wanted gang labor to produce the profits they had become accustomed to having. According to pbs.org, between 1910 and 1970, six and a half million blacks went to the north, leaving the cotton fields, and sharecropping behind. With the mechanization of farming and AMS leaving the south, sharecropping came to an end.

The quest for social justice came not just from the desires of the oppressed but some members of the former slave master's race demanded it as well. Today's version of sharecropping appears to be selective-ism...a word that has some roots in Charles Darwin's theory of survival of the fittest. The word is used to express how

American Caucasians apparently work to ensure the continued degradation of the AMS race; while simultaneously repelling their attempts to rise above economic oppression. It goes beyond degradation. As in the case of sharecropping, the former oppressors sought self-protection, survival, and fulfillment of selfish goals to the detriment of an already oppressed group of people. The mainstream society initiated programs such as affirmative action as a feigned attempt to correct some of the consequences of slavery and oppression.

Selective-ism involves choosing qualified and unqualified individuals to represent a larger group of people; and in doing so, the successes, shortcomings and failings of a few inaccurately represent the whole. The qualified individuals represent the fairness of the system; and each individual failure makes a statement that American society tried but those chosen and their people reveal that they don't have the necessary skills for success. It is a strategy in place with the current AMS President of the United States. See how far we have come as a country in electing an AMS to the presidency. History needs to reflect that his tenure has met the most uncompromising, belligerent group of white Republicans in the history of United States governance. See, we gave him a chance but he couldn't motivate racists, self-indulgent white guys to make a sacrifice for their country; in these difficult economic times. Therefore, any elected minority President will never have the full support of all the people...especially the Caucasians. The solution to that problem is to keep electing minority Presidents until they get used to it and change.

We are being told that victory at all costs means slow progress for the country; failure or mediocrity for the democratic politicians, and hero-status among some uncompromising political groups. Even when you give those AMS a chance, they simply don't try hard enough. When in reality, the system does the choosing and has never been fair. It can't really be fair while his or her great-grandparents owned the businesses and their cousins' cousins' cousins have worked for the family for generations; as well as friends of the cousin's fraternity brothers and politicians.

It is selective-ism that has allowed desperate, sycophant politicians to pull the "race card" of social injustices (food stamps, public handouts) when the majority of those on the dole are white folks. Selective-ism has developed the image of the needy AMS community but the times have dictated that many other races have now joined the tumult of economic depravity. It is a consequence of having a unified nation that many weak, selfish politicians don't understand: a rising tide does impact us all; but so does a sinking ship. Welcome to the new economic principles for 2012 and beyond.

Is the predicament of AMS its own fault? In taking a look at Brazil, the home of the 2014 World Cup, we see similar situations for the descendants of slaves. In a July 10, 2014 article by Roques Planas, it is pointed out that "Brazil imported more slaves between the 16th and 19th centuries than any other country..." in the Western Hemisphere.

They didn't have a civil rights movement but they have made it a constitutional right of these descendants of African slaves to own land. Those are the differences in the sojourn of our fellow descendants and AMS in America.

These black Brazilians also fill the jails disproportionately. The black Brazilians live in the worst housing and their children attend the poorest schools. Sounds familiar?

Incarceration, Lynching, and Other Acts of Terrorism

The last lynching occurred in the United States in Mobile, Alabama. The victim, Michael Donald, 19, was randomly picked by two members of the Ku Klux Klan. This is one element of second-class citizenry that a younger generation cannot understand. An AMS could walk down the street going to the store and get apprehended by white folks who wanted to entertain themselves by taking the life of an innocent brother.

The young Michael Donald was hanged on a tree within view of Henry Hays' house. James Knowles, the other Klan member and murderer, and Mr. Hays, kidnapped the teenage Mr. Donald at gunpoint, beat him, and slit his throat. That was the last recorded lynching in America. This murder happened surprisingly in March 1981.

In the less than a twenty-year span of time following 1889, more than 2400 people of African descent were hanged or burned at the stake. Lynching was often publicized and a carnival-like atmosphere was created (children were encouraged to watch) around these horrendous events. People were usually never punished or charged and this had to encourage the continuation of such barbarous events. Sometimes, the impetus for such disasters was often a dark-skinned citizen acting out of character for which the former oppressors had slated them. These African Americans were acting "out of place or uppity" or competing for jobs or making boastful remarks about rising against oppression, seeking to better himself, or telling a white person the truth. The underlying theme was lynching to control, intimidate, and manipulate a group of people into living under fear.

According to *The Negro Holocaust: Lynching and Race Riots in the United States,1880-1950,* by Robert A. Gibson, the NAACP "sponsored anti-lynching legislation such as the Dyer Anti-Lynching Bill and numerous other proposals to make lynching a federal crime." Of course, white politicians argued that such legislation would infringe upon states' rights and no legislation was passed. This alone implies a state's right to lynch African Americans without due process and a lack of commitment of the government to protect all of its citizens. Once again, an argument for reparations.

The great state of Oklahoma is well-known for various forms of intimidation against AMS. The famous picture of Laura Nelson hanging from a bridge in a dress has been published many times. She had tried to protect her son who was hanged with her. After lynching AMS farmers, the land would often be confiscated by whites. So, not only was lynching used to dissuade AMS from voting; it was a method of thievery; and continued generational suppression of a race of people. Again, slavery was tortuous but capitalistic oppression, keeping us from the American Dream after offering us nothing for our suffering, has had an ongoing impact.

Then, by the awesome power of integration, a more powerful form of lynching came into prevailing dominance. Incarceration has been a more humane method for keeping a race of people economically oppressed and mentally depressed. We have to face the facts that our current justice system is empowered at the roots by generations of police officers and judicial officials who have often disliked American Souls; and have bought into a system that condones the unfair treatment of people to support America's capitalistic ways.

In other words, our justice system is designed to perpetuate second-class citizenry. In the racist, oppressive system, the police officers select who will fill the slots for this economic and political travesty. That is why "stop and frisk laws" must be condemned in New York.

In effect, the country transitioned shakily from slavery to sharecropping, to Jim Crow, to economic enslavement. Every step of the way, the AMS were treated as if they were not a part of building this country; and we had more naturalized rights (based on birth land and centuries of blood) than immigrants in the years following slavery. But we were perceived as a threat partially because of injustices performed against us and the expectation of revenge. Partially, because of a longing to keep things as they had been. So, we had informal and formal laws upheld against us until we had little expectation of being a true part of this country.

Some police officers still select and ensure entry-level participants for the oppressively brutal, second-class citizenry machine. They become jaded by urban crime and the dark and brown faces being herded into squad cars. The officers play guessing games regarding the alleged criminal's description, including age and culture. Although, they rarely relate this cultural bias to the relevant facts that these suspects' ancestors have been abused to fit into a criminal niche that lures generations of potential resources from this country. That is not their job, of course. They simply make the arrests, with a bias that would take Sigmund Freud quite some time to elucidate.

So pervasive is the systematic bias that Mayor Bloomberg foolishly announced on June 28, 2013 that: "Nobody racially profiles." His argument was based on the fact of less white folks committing crimes while a greater percentage of whites get stopped. So, whites commit 7 percent of the crimes and get stopped 9 percent of the time; although they carry 44% of the guns.

In 2012, of the over 533,000 stops, 87% were American Soul and Latinos. I'm sure that the high rate of frisking people once they were stopped has to do with stereotypes and some cultural bias among law enforcement. The systemic racist machine is in full-swing and the detrimental effects are self-perpetuating. Law enforcement has some difficulty distinguishing possible culprits from highly unlikely AMS citizens; so, all sorts of people get stopped.

It is not the police officer's job to categorize criminals but he or she must be able to effectively perform job responsibilities within the cultural, social, and commonsense boundaries relevant for communities for which he or she serves.

In policing the streets of New York, one can see how much more effective it would be if police officers were trained to apply some of the same principles of respect, that are performed with other citizens. It is wise to use good reasoning skills prior to stopping a 55 year-old man dressed in a suit, walking in the opposite direction of the reported criminal's escape route.

The act of arresting minorities for minor infractions and for no probable cause, appears to make a great deal of sense for heading off the tidal wave of urban crime but in reality it creates other problems, including trust issues.

These biased and illegal arrests (proven illegal) raise the statistics of AMS arrests and confirms for society the identity of the suspected threat: it's those black folks. Should the mayor ignore the racial undertones of stop and frisk: ignoring the fact that in urban areas a larger number of minorities in a youthful age range, acquiesce to police authority and in effect give permission to be searched? Centuries of law enforcement/governmental abuse brings out our PTSD and we are wise enough to do what the authorities request with no drama. When we start shouting, "You don't have probable cause, Officer!" we could have several witnesses and a video camera rolling; and end up charged with several crimes.

Is the mayor prepared to ignore the fact that most cops, including AMS, have a tendency to believe certain crimes are perpetrated by AMS between specific ages; so, they internalize the wager machine of their soul, guessing where the criminal will be found, what he will be wearing, and the color of his skin? Black neighborhoods are not as homogenous economically as Caucasian communities. The middle-class still tends to reside near or with the economically lower-class. So, law enforcement will often encounter or cross paths with the middle-class AMS while searching for the criminal of darker hue; and yes, sometimes the criminal will be the children of the middle-class.

Who cares for the child once adults with drug problems or other criminal offenses have been all locked up? Does a brilliant child with criminally-negligent parents do just as well or better with the parent incarcerated? Should the system put a brother in jail to rehabilitate him and remove him from some temptations? What happens when the young man interacts with seasoned criminals, and is kept from saving money and counseling his children and loving his wife? We get instability on so many levels. And we still have the data that shows that sympathy before the judge and jury is mainly reserved for white folks. Does this provide for a healthy transition to trusting America's justice system, after slavery, after Jim Crow, after the death of King, Evers, Chaney, Goodman, and Schwerner, and the attacks against economic empowerment?

The police officers and prison guards rarely see the light of hope. They see the new lows of society's moral turpitude; and many become jaded.

In Illinois, a police officer was charged with beating confessions out of suspects in the 80's and 90's (of course we can go back to the 40's, 30's, 20's…etc. with others). Already the authority among PTSD AMS, police officers can threaten to pull out every offense, add a few, and prognosticate how poorly the jury will perceive a black citizen; and throw in a few punches, while providing the citizen with the opportunity for police leniency if he confesses.

Also in this state, a brother who made furniture in prison and received a day's wage for a month in prison ($75) was told that he needed to pay restitution for his time in prison. The man had been convicted of murder, served his time, and had established a savings of over $10,000. Any semblance of making it through and out of the system often initiates an all-out assault from the system's more devious members; hence the excuse for the systemic degradation of financial empowerment.

He has a daughter who could use the money and perhaps a generation would be empowered. Or he may get out of jail and the funds would help to keep him from doing something he may deem necessary, but if caught it would send him back to jail. Why do we continue to support an American justice system that still seems geared towards keeping 'just us' oppressed? In 2014, there are approximately 2 million people incarcerated in local, state, and federal prisons in this wonderful country. China, with four times the population as the United States, has about 1.6 million citizens incarcerated. AMS and the black and the brown, are most likely to feel this economic unfairness or double punishment because we are the ones filling the prisons.

The state of Georgia has been involved in a great number of civil rights issues; and it has produced great leaders among AMS. The state is home to two infamous cases where two AMS high school athletes, in two separate incidents, were charged with rape after having consensual sex with white girls; and the state of Georgia brought the gavel down upon them with 10-year sentences.

Tell me if I'm wrong but I haven't heard of white guys having sex at 17-years of age in high school, and going to jail. AMS mothers in Georgia had better watch out when your son's birthday comes early; and he is popular, and having sex, because chances are, some innocent-looking, sweet 15-16 year old will allow him to have sex with her. One of the aforementioned young men was Marcus Dixon, now a superstar with the New York Jets. He got out after serving 15 months in a Georgia prison.

The other guy is Genarlow Wilson. He's not 6'4" like Mr. Dixon but he actually had more of a right to be free. The girl initiated the sex with her fellow student; and although she was 15 years old, he was only 17 years old in 2005. He was released on October 26, 2007 from the Burrus Correctional Training Facility after the Georgia State Supreme Court ruled that Wilson's sentence was cruel and unusual. He served more than 2 years of a 10-year sentence. His goal was not to take a plea deal like other guys in the "hotel party" because he did not want to be a registered sex offender and suffer penalties for life.

So, how do we pay as a nation for the tremendous loss of human resources? How do we dismiss the generations of mistrust and needless injustices? The United States has the highest documented prison population in the world at 754 persons imprisoned per 100k. AMS comprises about 12% of the United States population and about 38% of the US prison population. It appears that we are a threat to somebody; and somebody wants to limit our input in mainstream society. But the greatest threat is wrought by the injustices and loss of human potential. We pay the price as a people; and so does the country.

April 24, 2013
The Art of Living Black

They didn't care...and the they that came after them didn't care. They used the words "emancipated" and "freemen" but in reality it was a bureaucratic shuffle from solitary confinement to the general population. Four million slaves freed with no jobs, little to no literary and linguistic skills; and hated by the ruling white authority among which they had to seek employment. All dressed up with no place to go. The abolitionists and fair-minded folks couldn't possibly take care of the vast numbers of freed people. Imagine some people searching for family members, all needing food and shelter and jobs; while none are available. We learned to do without, to pray, to help each other, and to make do with little. We accepted our dilemma and many did whatever was necessary to make a living. They broke the law and took what was deemed as necessary risks in order to make a life worth living in America.

Some AMS with high moral standards chose a conservative, crime-free lifestyle. But they knew the dilemma that society placed on us and they empathized with those who did whatever it took to eke out a living in freedom.

People say slavery has no impact on today. In my hometown, the drug dealer who sold heroin smiled and waved at all the people going to church; and the church folk waved back and asked him to join them. He owned a bar and sold drugs and no one snitched because we were in effect fighting against a common enemy and some were assigned assassins.

I was puzzled by my father's nonchalant acceptance of the gambling house that was housed in one of his rental properties. As a child I clearly saw the conflict: he was a deacon of the church and we went to church several times a week. Those criminals of the past didn't directly kill people; they survived and promoted survival.

"A man's gotta do what a man's gotta do," my father answered when I questioned why he allowed it to be.

I assume when cocaine really flourished the profits were too high for people to remain cordial to each other. Now no snitching translates into communities impoverished and clouded by hails of bullets; not to mention the terrible toll of addiction crossing all economic and cultural walls.

What's worse? Having your life ruined by years in prison so that you walk around with a prison mentality and limited opportunities... or making prison your home; replete with corruption, sex, and illegal enterprises. Thirteen female Maryland state prison guards were charged with a federal racketeering indictment as they all but relinquished control of the prison to a gang.

They legally worked for the State of Maryland but their prison mentality seduced them to work for the prisoners. The incarcerated Black Guerilla Family gang members were allowed to obtain sex, drugs, and various contraband in order to facilitate their illegal enterprises in prison and out of prison. In doing so, the had-to-be charismatic leader, Tavon White, impregnated four of the guards. Two of them had his name tattooed on their bodies. Okay, who came up with the great idea to have heterosexual female guards supervise male prisoners? And, if allowed to watch these prisoners, someone needed to have an inferiority complex-meter to measure the tremendous insecurities these women had to emanate prior to the completion of ninety days of working; including how the uniforms impacted their femininity. Maybe they had something to prove.

Raise your hand if you think half a man is better than no man at all. Now raise your hand if you think your livelihood and a large portion of your life will not be ruined if you are paid to guard prisoners, but you have sex with a prisoner and get pregnant; and you help the prisoner to operate his criminal enterprise as you make plans to take care of the baby growing inside of you. What in the world were these four ladies thinking? It is the standard by which many of us still live. We live as if it is still *us* against *them*.

Mistrust and hopelessness are the byproducts of living and working within a system that systematically discounts your value. Television, movies, advertising, high-end restaurants, and high-paying jobs, all send the message that we don't belong in a certain economic class. It is not a melting-pot message. Soul to pay.

Judicial and Social Injustice

Many AMS don't even realize that our greatest enemy has been the psychological oppression of fighting against the same great system that opens up opportunities for us: it is the democracy that lifts us and the duplicitous democracy by which we suffer. It was a difficult thing even for a child to listen to Officer Friendly programs that encouraged belief in the police after seeing them turn water hoses and dogs on large groups of protesting AMS. The system designed to protect and give voice to all Americans often protected adjacent communities better, while lording uneven justice among some friends and family members.

Many AMS have stories in which they watched the police administer unequal justice; and they watched the judicial system free white criminals and give harsh sentences to AMS innocents and criminals.

So, we suffered with the knowledge that the judicial system would not support us if we defended ourselves with the violence threatened upon us. We knew that adult white bullies and thugs were buoyed by the system from arrest to conviction and a bullied AMS could be killed at any step in the process.

In the 1960's, I watched my daddy get cursed out and called "boy" by a much younger Georgia gas station attendant. He had to use the bathroom and the man made it clear that although no sign was displayed, no coloreds were allowed to use the public restroom. It brought an understanding of the complexities of accepted white oppression when years later, my family was fishing on Lake Winterset. My father was in the rear and my mother was in the front part of the boat. A group of three drunk white guys swirled around us so that their wake shook up and rocked our little 12-foot dinghy. One threw an empty can into our boat.

My father boldly stood up and cocked his rifle and I believed he would have shot them if necessary and so did they. They immediately turned their boats away and quickly left us alone. I remember thinking that white folks don't take that and they would be back but they never returned. I was worried about my father going to jail even though he was just defending his family.

Fast-forward to June 12, 2013. It has often been the Supreme Court's focus to bring justice when tyrants of the judicial system lorded over communities with their personal brand of justice. Chief Justice of the Supreme Court Judge John Roberts ordered a disciplinary review of Judge Edith Jones of the 5th Circuit Court of Appeals. She has come under a review for making allegedly racist and discriminatory remarks in a February 20th speech at the University of Pennsylvania Law School.

The complaint against her states that she said certain "racial groups like African-Americans and Hispanics are predisposed to crime," and they are "prone to commit acts of violence" and be involved in more "heinous" crimes than people representing other ethnic groups. She made some more questionable comments about Mexicans. Are white folks predisposed to violent acts spurred by a superiority-complex since they enslaved a race of people and developed informal and formal laws to support the travesty; dropped two Atomic bombs on Japan, and invaded a Middle Eastern country based on inaccurate information?

We can assume Judge Jones is an intelligent woman but the ignorance of her comments are exasperating. AMS can understand the red-neck, back-woods racist but one who sits on the bench in judgment of many of our people calls for a review of her past cases involving people of color. And again, the system gets bogged down with nonsense.

She went to law school in Texas; the same place where they want to change the history books to marginalize slavery.

Life isn't that bad most AMS would say. And that Caucasian conservative I spoke to recently asked me to explain how some successful blacks made it through if the system was so prejudiced against blacks.

Poor communities understood economic empowerment by any means necessary. And Caucasians understood it as well. What happens if those enslaved Negroes become free, and through hard work and perseverance reverse the socio-economic landscape? The history books would be rewritten Texas, but they would speak in glowing terms of a formerly enslaved group of people who persevered and made this country the ideal of what its founding fathers wrote on paper.

In 1831, Reverend Nat Turner led a slave rebellion that killed between 50-60 white men, women, and children. He believed that God had shown him signs to rebel against oppression and kill those who were carrying out the injustice of slavery. The slave rebellion was quickly suppressed but white folks retaliated as rumors spread about slaves killing families of plantation owners throughout the South. Many innocent slaves had to face the increased moral depravity of being killed simply out of fear. There were many other slave revolts; two occurred on ships: the Amistad and the Creole.

So, you can do what you will to a people but their retaliation will cause greater subjugation. "So shall we add tenfold thereto…" The theme followed AMS into post-slavery lifestyles. When black communities thrived they were in effect retaliating against economic oppression. There were numerous riots and violent acts perpetrated against AMS mainly because some black communities were thriving.

The Tulsa Race Riots, also known as the Greenwood Massacre (June 1, 1921), are an example of how a little ignorance mixed with fear can be extremely destructive. But it is also an example of how AMS sought and achieved economic empowerment and mainstream America envied our success to the point of destruction.

Supposedly, a misunderstanding occurred when a black man, Dick Rowland, came running out of an elevator while the white woman elevator operator screamed. This was assumed to be some type of sexual assault that was never proven and never caused any charges to be brought forth. He could have sneezed; or been pushed and accidentally touched her upon losing his balance; or he could have looked at her and smiled which at the time may have caused the woman some personal outrage.

An article by the Tulsa Historical Society states that Sarah Paige, the white elevator operator, claimed that Mr. Rowland grabbed her arm. The most common explanation for the scream is that he stepped on her foot as he entered the elevator (according to the Encyclopedia of Oklahoma History and Culture). Unfortunately, the ensuing chaos, based on hyped emotions, caused several deaths and considerable property damage.

Mr. Rowland was arrested. The rush to judgment by white folks, in the form of a lynch mob, was faced with opposition and protection by AMS; some of which were veterans of WWI. Some of them had guns and were prepared to defend Mr. Rowland against getting lynched. They offered assistance to the sheriff for the protection of Mr. Rowland; and the sheriff turned them down. Of course, some white folks were upset at seeing armed AMS and as they passed returning to their community, a confrontation took place and a shot was fired. The AMS community which was one of the most successful in the country at the time, was replete with newspaper publishers, churches and black-owned businesses.

On June 1, 1921, over one-thousand homes and businesses were destroyed as the state of Oklahoma's second largest AMS community was burned to the ground. The destruction caused by the riots was a tremendous setback for AMS as well as the nation. The governor declared martial law and 6000 members of the prestigious community, and all black Tulsans, were interned in the Convention Hall and Fairgrounds. According to the Tulsa Historical

Society, some were there for as long as eight days. Reports state 30-40 deaths; but a recent report states it was closer to 300 deaths and most of them AMS.

The race riot of New York in 1863 was known at the time as Draft Week. It started as a protest by working-class whites (mainly Irish men) against wealthier citizens being able to pay $300 to exempt them from the draft for the American Civil War. Free black men and immigrants competed for low-wage paying jobs in the city. Since black men were not considered citizens at the time, they were not obligated to fight for the country. The protest led to the working class men murdering over 100 blacks and destroying public property, homes, and churches.

In 1887 a race riot took place at a sugar plantation in Louisiana as thousands of sugar plantation workers (mostly black) went on strike. The East St. Louis Riot of 1917 and the Chicago Riots of 1919 grew out of job tensions between whites and AMS. Riots also occurred in the Atlanta Riots in 1906 and Omaha in 1919. As white folks were not accustomed to AMS having opinions about their well-being, they became offended at any expression of equality.

If there ever was a clear case for reparations it is the fact that during economic empowerment, AMS made great strides to lift ourselves out of the depravation caused by slavery. As our great efforts to excel in this country came to fruition, mainstream America, and the legal systems (local, state, and federal), and individual gun-toting rednecks, established harsher efforts to squelch economic growth. We learned to not be so successful as to draw attention to ourselves.

According to an article on BlackAmericanWeb.com by Nicole Kenney (February 6, 2013), "From the end of Reconstruction until WWI, falsely imprisoned blacks were leased to small-town entrepreneurs, provincial farmers, and corporations looking for abundant, cheap labor. In addition, fear, intimidation and even death (ownership was one of the primary causes for lynching) were employed against blacks for attempting to secure any type of socioeconomic mobility for themselves and their families. This country was evolving into a world-class economic superpower from the capital generated from slavery and Jim Crow policies and any accumulation of wealth by blacks that decreased the labor force would not be tolerated."

My father, Handy Stephens, owned property throughout central Florida. His nuclear family and some close relatives traveled from Marianna, Florida to central Florida for job opportunities. His father drove a wood wagon and delivered wood to the phosphate mines that were in construction. I surmised that my father didn't like that kind of work because he delivered orders for local pharmaceutical stores on his bicycle. One day, he made a delivery to a house that had had a live-in young servant woman named Lillie to whom he proposed and later married in March, 1934.

During his journeys, he also met a man named Jack Powell who owned a local gas station. It was Jack that my father credited with giving him a start in real estate. Eventually, my father owned and maintained ten houses and apartments in town; two houses in Gardenville (a suburb); and one duplex in Lake Wales, Florida. He had a seventh-grade education and always seemed to have the potential for being so much greater. When Jack Powell died, my father was the only African American who was present at the funeral. He was honored to be a pallbearer.

The help that my father received was a financial kick start. Mr. Powell could have asked for interest or some other form of repayment for assisting my father. But he did not lord over my father and he did not offer him special types of services from the gas station.

Somebody came up with affirmative-action to keep second-class citizenry alive in America. Even if a substantial but not break-the-bank financial settlement had been given to African Americans, it would have worked towards making things right.

I can see the meeting for this fiasco. Isn't it unconstitutional to provide breaks for blacks at the expense of better qualified whites? Of course it is, but by the time it gets through the court-system we would have done so much for the black race; and we can feel good about trying to do something. Why don't we give them reparations and be done with it? Are you kidding? Financing the needs of blacks on the backs of white folks' taxes? We might have a revolt on our hands. And many black folks will become extremely successful, putting us to shame for our past misdeeds.

In a sense, the fact that affirmative action programs were created, validates the fact that America is aware of its debt owed to AMS. The country could not or would not choose to resolve the situation by compensating the descendants of slaves (reparations) so, political leaders decided to provide exceptions for us in the struggle to assimilate and become economically successful.

After affirmative action was ruled unconstitutional (so was slavery) the country chose to ignore the continuing inequities established and nurtured by a wicked society. Well, that couldn't work so let's just ignore it and not do anything else. In a bending over backwards perspective, America owes AMS for the unconstitutional time frame in which we were forced to live as second-class citizens, faced lynching and illegal destruction to our communities due to physical violence and lack of the fair application of tax revenue. Due to racial prejudices, we were not allowed to benefit in the same way other citizens were allowed to benefit: our taxes were misappropriated as were services provided by various government programs.

That's what makes jokes by Kansas House Speaker Mike O'Neal appear to initiate a political race riot. He referred to Mrs. Obama as Mrs. YoMama and of course he later apologized according to an article in the Huffington Post.

The email had in the subject, "Twins separated at birth?" and it showed a picture of the Grinch next to a picture of Mrs. Obama. Mr. O'Neal made a comment as to how funny he thought the email was and he just had to share it.

Yet, on the following Thursday he apologized to those he offended; stating again that the picture made him laugh. These guys don't get AMS culture. Sure, rappers go around using derogatory words for our women but public and personal, disrespecting a brother's woman is worthy of a butt-whipping. As a matter of fact, talking about a man's woman for no reason, publicly, is considered rather unmanly---with no reference to any member of the LBGT.

That brings us to another weasel of a man: Rep. Jim Sensenbrenner (R-Wis.). He actually made a public comment about another man's wife's butt; saying she has a "large posterior" and "big butt." What is that fool looking for when he casts his sinful eyes back there...a small, flat butt? I am sure that the President is pleased; and if not, he better act like he is. When did America become so crass that we go around making comments about the First Lady's body parts? No man goes around publicly dissing anybody's wife's butt. Little weasels do it all the time, apparently.

Marilyn Davenport, an elected member of the Orange County, Calif., Republican Central Committee, forwarded an email picturing President Barack Obama's face on the body of a baby chimpanzee in April. This hussy refused to apologize and now it appears that these white folks have issues with the features of public leaders who don't happen to have pale features and other body parts that they deem as the best. Yes, oh the pain of the insecure ways of insecure, race-baiting nitwits.

AMS know this scam. As human beings, these are highly-sensitive emotional issues and most people would react with a highly emotional response; but an AMS woman (especially one in the limelight) would immediately be labeled as "an angry black woman" and would fit into the stereotype that has been permeated since slavery was abolished. We bear the insults of generations of race-baiting simply because we are ethnically different and we can't even show anger when insulted. Well, I can; and I'm angry.

Oddly, the anthems and numerous songs, and accomplishments of our people over the years have worked. We like our looks. We perceive how God sculptured us and most of us, like the rest of the peoples of the world, have come to understand individual attributes and enjoy it.

Yes, I get angry...and righteous indignation is accepted as a proper response to injustice. But the system is aware that the AMS race has more of a right for this response than anyone and they fear it; so, we polite, level-headed folks stay cool, calm, and collected. We don't like labels.

It is a unique characterization of America as the land of the free; or at least it has been. These days the phrase rings prophetic utterance---citing the reason for the demise of the country. Can there really exist such a thing as too much freedom? Wasn't it our expectation of supremacy and sense of aloofness that prompted us to think that no one would seek to terrorize our powerful, capitalistic, militaristic, principled country? So we puffed up our chest and failed to take necessary precautions against terrorists. We learned at such a great cost that some freedoms are worth the price and sacrifice of time, money, and human capital needed to remain diligent.

It is almost intimidation to say that your soul will pay; or has paid for past sins. What arrogance! What a musical chairs-style prophetic declaration of retribution for sinful western living. Anything that happens within the lifetime after these words can be met with, "I told you so. Vengeance is mine, sayeth the Lord." But there are some things that take generations to manifest. They come from the bowels of poor decisions and deceptions; covered with the perfume of self-righteousness. They stink from the beginning but just like the Emperor's New Clothes, people gather around and pretend not to see the truth until the majority of people agree on the unrighteousness of the wrong.

It is our dilemma to decide justified outrage at occurrences in modern times. Are we victims so much so that we relive past injustices or are we facing an evil (American racism) that has grown extra legs and greater mind power to continue to persecute people of different hues. The Tea Party appears to exist as an example of this hybrid of ugly. Some shout the racist n-word but most simply use the rhetoric of anger towards different opinions.

They speak with the voice of post-Civil War whites who feared white supremacy would be jeopardized by AMS equality. It is a new day but politicians speak against the President as no one has ever spoken before. They speak revolution without considering the consequences. They speak as if in a glass bubble where their collective voices will not influence the prosperous, the simple-minded, the violent, and the misinformed. And upon occasion, when someone gets hurt (as in the shooting of Gabrielle Giffords and others in Arizona) they will proclaim their right to say whatever they desire without regard to disastrous consequences that often accompany adamant advocates of governmental revolution.

Stop "Stop and Frisk" in New York

The new radical, declining majority ignores the capitalistic, judicial, and governmental system which places large numbers of AMS in prisons. Instead, they concentrate on the AMS outcry for justice as whining. We are psychologically muzzled. But as momma used to say: "It is the squeaky wheel that gets the oil." We should care less about the improper disposition of certain right-wing paranoid racist interactions that belittle us and often leaves us empty, as some majority members of society state: "see, they were wrong again...those people complain too much."

With so many AMS thrown in prison, you would think the ruling class has enough oppressive social, political, ideological, and psychological vehicles to suppress the rising of the minority class. You would not think that they would continue to oppress us by profiling us and stopping us on the sidewalks, frisking us, and arresting us. It surely increases the odds of attaining a higher arrest record and incarceration rate among AMS. The "Stop and Frisk" policy ensures a large number of AMS in jail and it confirms for the fair-minded that AMS are at the core of criminality in America. I like the way New York Police Commissioner Ray Kelly puts it: the AMS and Latino community are being victimized by AMS and Latino criminals. As the officers patrol these communities, the officers stop and frisk in order to upend a crime or crime wave. The data does not support the policy no matter how practical it sounds. The New York Times reports that in 2002, when Ray Kelly took office, 97,246 people were violated by "stop and frisk." 587 homicides were reported. In 2011, those numbers increased almost six-fold to 685,724; with a nice decrease in murders to 532. In one neighborhood, 93 out of 100 residents have been stopped and frisked. The commissioner says that it is the most diverse police force in America; but what is being done to eradicate racism; not pander to it. The police are supposed to have reasonable suspicion and "must be able to point to specific and articulable facts; so, most stop and frisk arrests are unconstitutional. Carl Dix explains in an October 21, 2011 AOL article, "Why I Am Getting Arrested Today," that an unjustified stop and search which resulted in his being detained in 1961 is still going on today. Mr. Dix is a writer, speaker, and founding member of The Revolutionary Communist Party, USA. Although, I cannot separate the issue from the politics and neither am I concerned with that, for me, this issue is about racial injustice and not communism as a solution.

With such tactics, America strips itself of generations of human resources. Innovative "idea men", creative artists, scientists, philosophers, and mathematicians, all are taken away for years; keeping them away from nurturing their families and families to be. Just as AMS has to squelch our mindset of us against them, to make this country great again, they need to consider AMS as resources. Sure, the country will eventually change its face as Hispanic minorities are projected to gain majority status and intermarriage occurs within the races; but the country will grow, strengthen, and benefit all.

(Details about the following were first posted on Huffington Post 2/7/2012. No author listed.)

Predictably, the extra confrontation with police via stop and frisk led to the murder of an 18-year old male. Ramarley Graham was running from police officers when he ran into his grandmother's home. He ran into the bathroom and it is speculated that he was attempting to flush marijuana down the toilet.

Enter (illegally) the frustrated, pursuing, NYPD officer Richard Haste, age 30. He goes to the bathroom in grandma's apartment and shoots the unarmed Ramarley Graham. Here is a man-child, murdered (in an unlawful entry and search), for carrying dope and not allowing himself to be caught by a frustrated cop. The case is unwinnable after the evidence is flushed; and the officer has to admit a type of defeat...but he has the authority and the gun, so he shoots as if to make the criminal pay for taking up his valuable time and for daring to think that he knew the law well enough to avoid paying for such a minor infraction. The officer had to feel as if the boy had beat him. Different neighborhood, different color, and the boy lives; because the police officer will have an excuse to calm down; the boy looks like him and could have been his son.

Of course, the lies and the misinformation came forth to taint the innocence of the victim. Most are guilty of something but death is not the penalty for their criminal offenses. The word was leaked that Ramarley wrestled with a police officer in the apartment building prior to going to the bathroom. The intent, I assume, was to make it more plausible to shoot an unarmed suspect who was aggressively resisting arrest. But this scenario also makes it questionable as to why would you shoot someone with whom you have had a close, non-life-threatening experience. That lie had to be dropped.

Monday, June 11, 2012, Officer Richard Haste was indicted on manslaughter charges in the death of Ramarley Graham. August 8, 2013, a jury determined that there was not enough evidence to re-indict Richard Haste. The initial indictment was thrown out due to an error made by an assistant district attorney when presenting evidence to the grand jury.

August 12, 2013

A federal judge, Shira Scheindlin, ruled that the stop and frisk policy to thwart crime in New York was itself a violation of the rights of thousands of New Yorkers. She called for a federal monitor to supervise the changes to the policy that intentionally discriminates based on race.

It is not as if this is new information. The violation had to be known since inception. The proud citizens of New York are glad that this tremendous violation of an oppressed group of people has been removed; prior to it spreading and polluting other law enforcement agencies.

Accomplish One Goal and Someone Always Changes the Rules

Saturday evening, November 27, 2010

After the annual Harvard-Yale football game, some black alumni of both institutions gathered with others at a special invitation-affair outside of an exclusive New England club. "Management called the owner to say that they saw individuals on line whom they recognized as '*local gang bangers*,'" wrote event organizer and Harvard alum Michael Beal: "We were perceived as a threat because of our skin color."

Mr. Beal expressed the group's measures taken to ensure that the "bad seeds" (local gang-bangers) were not allowed in so the implication is that in a fair and just society, racial profiling would not be needed as unwanted people would be weeded out prior to specific events occurring.

This statement further explains the complexities of our problem. We know that we are different from social deviants who commit crimes but the truth is that it is easier for special groups (with low black membership) to use racial profiling as precautionary measures in ensuring the safety of the club; so what if a few nice, innocent people get discriminated against.

With this ease comes the slaughter of individual rights and the racist assumption that only black folks cause problems at exclusive affairs held inside clubs. Mr. Beal may not be able to see that the implication bolsters his sense of achievement: after all, isn't it so that African American alumni of Harvard and Yale will only be represented by one or two so any more than that will constitute a gang? Or have times continued to change so that by now there are a fair amount of alumni of these prestigious institutions and one cannot discriminate (racial profiling) to bolster insecure feelings about interaction of races?

Such incidents find us pleasingly surprised that African American alumni of Harvard and Yale exist. We know that there can only be but so many attending and we know that they did not look like gang-bangers by dress or ethnicity because gang-bangers come in all colors. Level heads should have prevailed. We understand the racism but we like to think that reasonable minds would come to a better conclusion than to call the local law enforcement on people based on the color of their skin.

The truth is that local gang bangers would probably not be interested in attending a party filled with the stuffed-shirts of such prestigious institutions. Yet, the establishment owners chose to close the facility rather than take the time to discover who was actually an alumnus of the institutions in question. Most assuredly, any minority alumnus would proudly bear the insignia, ring, card, or some form of identification that associates him with the institution.

Rates Limbaugh

Okay. It takes a great trial to induce sadness in me but it's sad to listen to Rush Limbaugh as he fans the fires of hatred, discord, and dissatisfaction without offering reasonable, fair-minded, solutions.

Before black folks can think about hating, he accuses AMS of hating this country; playing on the fears of conservative Caucasians. That is sad because all of my life I have rarely heard anyone say that they hate this country. I have heard statements regarding the poor treatment of AMS but I can say it is uncommon for AMS to say they hate this country. We actually view our ancestors' labor and torturous lives as an investment and justification for our right to possess certain aspects of this country. Rush Ratings Limbaugh has sold his soul for syndicated radio ratings and he makes statements about our feelings because that is the prospective of "the guilt-stricken, guilt-deferring, insecure and in charge."

Despite this country's ardent task to put more on us than we can bear, we actually look at ourselves as Americans; and we can't hate our country.

The scheme always covers a laundry list of pitiful subjects that alienate the majority from minorities. Extreme radio jocks associate socialism with welfare and reparations. They know that we are due certain benefits that White America kept from us even after freedom from slavery. We paid taxes but were denied better schools, books, and an equal education. Rush makes us out to be whiners with no reasoning, so that we won't whine while he muddles through issues of inequalities like a pig playing in the mud. He knows the pain and suffering caused by his ancestors upon our ancestors so he adds some slop and plays until other people get persuaded into thinking that it's fun to get filthy dirty.

Do we make claims against wrong in the country? Sure, sometimes; and he seeks to make us out as whiny by lying and saying that is what we want now. There is no secret agenda for what we want from this country. He can't even understand that so he makes it out to be some secret agenda; and this improves his ratings periodically. Trust us, Rate; we would want the world to know what is happening, what we want, and what action in which we want the world to engage with us.

Rush also seeks to pit AMS against the Asians. He frequently mentions how other minorities come over and succeed and those who were born in this country (sorry Rush but white folks were born here as well) can't seem to get it together without a handout. Wow! How observant of you Rush. The system has come against the AMS. The old boy network must prove that they are superior and that poor treatment of blacks was somehow warranted because they can't succeed as a people. He fails to mention that oppression of blacks has been well documented pass the time of slavery and civil rights legislation; until the present. He fails to point out that the system of slavery and Jim Crow was dependent upon keeping blacks illiterate. He fails to mention that upon getting jobs in our communities and paying taxes, we failed to get our fair share of tax benefits for schools and recreational facilities.   Rush   Limbaugh's spin does not belittle the African American community's fight against the prevailing standards of racism throughout American institutions.

Funny thing is that he says outlandish comments about race and culture and he remains on the air. As if he is the voice of militant white America. I'm beginning to sense a real conspiracy: rich, Caucasian males are assembling to keep themselves as an economic   majority despite the great efforts put out by the minorities.

Media, Power, and Race

How magnificent the power of media in 2013. The reason we have limited access to the media is due to its power. It is not racist that a few groups have control over specific forms of media. Specific groups make movies; former athletes have access to the radio and broadcasting; and a few black directors have a large following among AMS. We have community issues because we have not practiced the art of community except when we joined efforts to fight against white America's inclinations to exclude us from the American Dream. Now, in tough times, we need to maximize our brothers' and sisters' efforts in the media and not denigrate those who have slightly differing opinions from our own.

Don Lemon, an AMS, gay commentator on CNN, made a comment in support of a white commentator (Bill O'Reilly) and chastised the AMS community, saying what we should be doing. Not an uncommon act but one that should stop. No other ethnic group airs its laundry before the world. And to make matters worse, other AMS leaders and celebrities take to the media airwaves to criticize Mr. Lemon's critical statements.

We can't see the forest for the trees on this one. Martin Luther King and Malcolm X were walking think tanks that garnered worldwide respect and empowered listeners to action. Tavis Smiley has organized groups of AMS as think tanks and they have addressed numerous concerns of the AMS community. Mr. Lemon was attempting to address a few concerns of the community. But his affiliation to CNN clouded his presentation although I understood his points as expressing a need for moral direction. A national group of athletes (1 or 2), politicians, minsters, and entrepreneurs would do well to change our thoughts to aggressive organizers and increase our perception as a unified group that can be reached quickly and efficiently. This body of thinkers should change as powerful people arise periodically to take the worldwide spotlight.

An example of such a group might include Oprah, Dr. Cornel West, Ben Jealous, Bishop T D Jakes, Tyler Perry, Herman Cain, and Eric Holder. This group would vote on who else should join and establish some bylaws for making decisions and taking action. Yes, it is a bit ostentatious but we would need an immediate, established presence. Other ethnic groups assemble naturally and for various reasons, such inclinations escape us.

Rick Sanchez, a television commentator for CNN, was fired after a Sirius/XM radio interview in which he publicly denounced the powers that be; although he used an old racial stereotype of Jews in the media to support his rant. Now, I rarely listened to CNN for several reasons: first, my loyalty remains to the local news networks; and I fill the national ,void by means of the Internet; and secondly, I have questioned the obvious political slant of the network and its owner, Rupert Murdoch, who also owns Fox News...ugh. But one day I watched the program and I noticed this guy with a Spanish surname who looked like another white guy: I wondered what was he doing on the show?

Sanchez was among the many media personalities that Jon Stewart made fun of on "The Daily Show. I have often wondered about the feelings of Stewart's targets. It is almost as if these victims deserve an appearance on his show because of his skewering; although his victims often have a one-dimensional, divisive view of politics and often can't see the forest for the trees. I have heard Rick Sanchez and could not agree with much of what he says but his classic defense against Stewart's ribbing is an ironic tale that should be told again and again.

Unless you have been under a rock for the last twenty or thirty years, you know that CNN is a news network that operates 24 hours a day (founded by Ted Turner in 1980). If you heard something and are not sure about it, go to CNN and they will confirm their own version of the subject matter. You will feel the allure of a 24-hour intellectual tease; and then, and only then, will everything be as clear as muddy water. I am usually on the side of Jon Stewart and I love the jokes he makes (although some are very unforgiving). Perhaps, for the first time in Rick Sanchez's career, he faced the dilemma that all minority sellouts face: how much longer can I pretend that the value of this important job should be prioritized ahead of my cultural integrity?

Is it worth the condescending looks and jabs; sprinkled with the occasional confirming action and insult (the occasional minority jab that does not include you because you are not like them)? Rick Sanchez really is a minority; who works for a network that has been accused of racial bias in news-reporting. A network that will take innocent, real, colorful news and spin it until it's accusatory and bleached.

Based on Rick's reactions to Stewart's jabbing, I assume that Rick had played the game for so long that he forgot who he really was; and he had forgotten that the rage he takes home always has the potential to leak out at an inappropriate time; and people would know what he really thought about his "superiors."

Caucasians don't know the burden of our PTSD. We tone-down cultural vernacular and perspectives, speech patterns, attire, and habits so as not to offend them and to make them more comfortable. We have no clue as to the detrimental impact we place on ourselves and our families as they watch both sides of us walk in and out of the door. We wait until the wee hours of the morning to reflect and temporarily claim who we are supposed to be.

As a member of the community of AMS PTSD, we know that Rick Sanchez had dealt with the innuendos and the direct affronts that questioned his abilities, and he kept his angst hidden because at some places it is difficult to prove racial or cultural bias, and keep a comfortable working environment. Employers and coworkers will provide hints of their true feelings but when it comes to testifying, everyone really loves each other.

For Rick, the testimony of his job environment spoke volumes; CNN's slant often failed to empathize with minorities and liberal perspectives. Rick worked in a place among people whom he spoke to daily and with whom he had cordial relationships; but most of them probably could not appreciate the cultural diversity that had to make him a jewel among small segments of the population; and among Latin American countries. In his mind and career, he had arrived. But his soul felt slighted because he knew that his uniqueness among the white media bureaucracy also limited the manner in which his gifts could be utilized.

As he grew in confidence and respect in his career, they were not prepared for him and he would not be satisfied with stagnation; no matter how much money it paid. He wanted to exist as a total man, not as some shallow, manipulated copy of himself. He wanted his ethnicity to show in his speech, topics, food, dress, or whatever he was neglecting and suppressing among his so-called colleagues.

Minorities know that in the eyes of many, our culture is like a confirmation of only the negatives of us; yet, we love many of the things about our culture that others may consider too ethnic. Our culture then becomes a thing that we put on at specific moments among certain people, but this confirms our cowardice and our selling out. No one feels good about selling out their very cultural identity. Are minority broadcasters stereotyped by whites and some Jewish media moguls as not being as good as them? This for me is the most poignant moment of dealing with Rick Sanchez. He really is Hispanic; a minority. I thought that he was simply another rightwing conservative with a Hispanic surname.

Whoa! Brother Rick Sanchez came out of the cultural closet. This guy has made the quintessential statement for all minorities quietly functioning as "whitely" as possible in a professional environment. I love that Shaun Robinson on Access Hollywood because she shows her ethnicity and professionalism at the same time. In her role, she has an advantage because it is entertaining; she is beautiful and dark brown.

Rick Sanchez was trapped in a more serious venue with darts thrown at him while he got lost in the professionalism. Had he used his minority skills, he would have appreciated Jon Stewart joking him and did some ribbing of his own. Instead he flashed. His mind raced with the years of career slights; and with the looks and snide remarks that he still receives. He flashed with visions of others joking with Jon Stewart about him; including his bosses whom he imagined sipping tea or worshipping with Jon at a celebrity-filled synagogue. He flashed a confirmation that he would never be able to know all that goes on behind the sacred doors of ethnic flavor, and favor, because his enemy was a cultural brother of his employers (Jewish brothers and media moguls).

What is a rich minority who wants to get richer to do? Rick flashed as if he had to say something that has been eating at him since that time when he first experienced this anger. He is just like many of us. He has made concessions regarding race and racially-charged debates in order to keep from defending the indefensible. We can't defend the consequences of slavery simply because many minorities have risen above the circumstances. It would take a great mind to cover the innumerable variances of racial discrimination and slavery without appearing to make excuses.

We see the small nuisances of our communities that are a direct result of skin-color discrimination. We see the look that means I don't like your color, your people, and your speech patterns. We hear people acting out their racial perspectives of minority accents, dances, handshakes, music, and loving. We see it on advertising featuring animals talking, and we hear it out of the mouths of our supervisors. And we keep our mouths shut to get along and to keep our jobs; and to avoid moments like the ones experienced by Rick Sanchez.

Pete Dominic interviewed Rick and claimed that Stewart, who is Jewish, is a minority like Sanchez, but Sanchez didn't agree. He argued that the wealth and power of the Jewish community does not put them in the same boat as black and Hispanic people. During the interview, Sanchez stated that Stewart is a person with "a white liberal establishment point-of-view" who "can't relate to a guy like me." Sanchez also felt that Stewart was "upset that someone of my ilk is at, almost, his level." Rick was letting it out with this one because one thing minorities understand is that emotional unquantifiable outbursts can easily be misconstrued as whining or more akin to whining or making excuses for seeming inferiority; so here was his chance to qualify his statements.

Rick Sanchez stated: "I've known a lot of elite Northeast establishment liberals that may not use this as a business model, but deep down when they look at a guy like me they look at a – they see a guy automatically who belongs in the second tier and not the top tier." Again, members of the AMS community know the frustrating corner in to which Rick backed himself. No one can state definitively what someone is thinking; but we know what racist attitudes project.

"White folks usually don't see it. But we do – those of us who are minorities and women see it sometimes, too, from men in authority." Good idea to toss women in the barrel with us, Rick.

Rick, Rick, Rick; I really know that you are truly a brother now. We understand that statement; but you put yourself out there again. They (mainstream media, white folks, generous people) get offended when we tell them what they can't perceive or understand because it almost makes us sound superior in specific areas of human interaction and cultural diversity.

We have seen the pitiful lows of humanity in daily glimpses, in whispers, in poor treatment or partiality towards specific groups of people. Yes, we see it, Rick; but they don't and can't admit or perceive that it exists in multiple arenas. After all, admission of the problem would also indicate some responsibility for its development and solutions. Welcome back, Rick Sanchez; and I apologize because as far as I know, you never left. I prefer this angle: You have been liberated. Now, may God bless you as you go forth and seek another job.

Jewish people look white and have very few features that will distinguish them from being regular white people. If Jews were a minority, how come they represent three of the nine justices on the Supreme Court? Three Jewish men got together to form one of the most powerful, movie-making companies in the world. The Jewish influence in America alone cannot compare to the current status of real minorities, such as Hispanics and African Americans. Now, this doesn't mean that Jews have not suffered as much because in some ways they have suffered more and we do have a kinship as being discriminated against and persecuted for our differences.

With cultural PTSD, our varied differences perceive racial threats differently, and we react differently. A particular slur may impact me greater than another one; but someone else may have a more demonstrative reaction than I would because of the person's intent to hurt. We therefore needed to establish the standard that the words are offensive because they are offensive "...to the least of these." Stop using the N-word.

Yet, Rick Sanchez presented a problem we minorities always have to face: if we call it like we see it, we can be perceived as whiners, excuse-makers, or racially-insensitive towards white folks who don't want the issue broached. Funny thing: I can finally relate to Rick Sanchez and what he had to endure as a successful minority among the white media conservative machine that is CNN. Rick exhaled, and simply spoke the truth as he experienced it. Apparently CNN has some difficulty with handling the truth. Good for you, Sanchez. Go somewhere where you'll be appreciated for being you: an intelligent, well-spoken man who happens to be Hispanic.

During the week of October 18-22, news broadcaster and commentator, Juan Williams, was fired by Nation Public Radio. His blessings continued when he was hired by Fox News (that might be a stretch for us to consider being affiliated with Fox News as a blessing).

Williams worked for Strom Thurmond at one time and wrote the book, "**Eyes on the Prize: America's Civil Rights Years, 1954-1965**." Strom Thurmond of course was a pioneer-racist politician who near his death was found to be sampling the chocolate candy that he wanted to keep in his pocket and allow to melt. His AMS maid/housekeeper was so loved by him that he fathered a baby girl. And of course, those good old black folks kept the secret until it was near his time to meet God. He stood for so much of the real Dirty South, that I find it unjustifiable to allow him to keep his racist image without tainting it with the realism of his lustful desires.

Working for him had to look and sound like the antebellum South and slavery. But who am I to judge?

Juan Williams has been a controversial figure among his own people and his dilemma propelled him to the ranks of a national controversial figure. In layman's terms, he has said something that his white bosses cannot support without offending a large group of wealthy people. I hope he has another book coming out shortly to benefit from this publicity.

In a radio interview, Williams was honest enough to reveal how he truly felt about seeing people dressed in Islamic garb on an airplane. Remember, you can't be too honest in the New America; just like in the old. He admitted that seeing Islamic people on flights made him a little uneasy; like many of us today on trains and buses but more on planes. His employer, NPR, fired him for his candor and in the face of racist commentators such as Queen Beck and Boss Fade Limbaugh, you would think that his words would be appreciated. They were not meant to incite and appeared to be a sincere expression of the trepidation that many people feel.

Juan Williams has often angered me with his awkward conservative spin on matters that impact the AMS community. When racist white conservatives have a controversial issue, they roll out Mr. Williams to show that even some black folks feel the same way. Williams has been the conservative commentator on Fox News and the commentator on the progressive National Public Radio. Surely, it was only a matter of time before he exposed himself as being more of one than another. On Thursday October 22nd, he was reportedly offered a job with Fox Network for 3 years at $2 million.

What a happy ending for Mr. Williams. But he has opened a very thin unstable door: why is it that AMS can receive a verbal lynching at the hands of every fool in the media while talking about homosexuals and Muslims is off-limits? Some of my southern gentlemen friends will not like this but here it is: America is afraid of being unfair to another group of people so much that we go overboard in allowing; we actually promote. In other words, the historic unfairness and cruelty of slavery can't be the reason why AMS are suffering in America because we are fair to everybody else (homosexuals, Native Americans, Asians). It must be an ill-conceived perception that the white majority is unfair.

Next, this country respects and often fears passion. Americans fear the unknown potential passion of Muslims, while being unable to distinguish the law-abiding faithful from the extremists. We know that there is more than one extremist group with some terror cells all around the world. We know that they have made it clear not to have the image of Mohammed placed on any literature and they don't like to be criticized. Although Americans like to make money criticizing and making derogatory remarks based on race and not skillset (Rushitz Limber, Gleen Beek, and Sheet Handy), our hate-monger commentators seem to know not to mess with the Muslims too much.

Bill O'Reilly appeared on The View and made a statement that caused Whoopi Goldberg and Joy Behar to walk off the set. He stated that Muslims killed us on 911. They apparently felt it more thoughtful for him to say that radical factions of Muslims or Muslim extremists caused 911. I thought it was an overreaction; perhaps to keep the set safe from terror. A simple correction (which someone did offer) should have sufficed. Everyone wants to be fair to everyone else but I am still wondering, where are my reparations?

October 20, 2010

Today, the Virginia GOP chairman, Dave Bartholomew, resigned after it was disclosed that he forwarded a racist email that compared blacks to dogs. In paraphrasing, the man's dog was described as *"black, unemployed, lazy, can't speak English and has no frigging clue who his Daddy is"* and needing to qualify for unemployment in order to get a check. After those qualifications, the man says his dog is getting a check on Friday. Of course, we are not supposed to wonder about the GOP being the harbinger of covert and overt racism in America. Again, such comments also reflect the harsh insensitivity of many Americans. Duh? African-Americans were brought here and kept here as slaves because we worked like crazy in the hot sun while white folks sipped on lemonade and had sex with slave women. They didn't want us to read for fear of being more capable of escaping; they wanted strong children for slavery for generations so they bred us. They promoted promiscuity and lack of family attachment. Then, the former oppressor refused to give us good jobs, even when qualified; so, we found it extremely difficult to take care of our families. What in the world is this fool talking about. What does this say for the GOP in Virginia?

With the anonymity of online communications, some people will express deeply held rude, racist beliefs that they would otherwise keep under wraps. Some people say AMS should have been glad that our ancestors were enslaved because it allowed us to come here. Some say stop whining and leave the past in the past. But clearly, the past is still present and AMS feel the impact of racist attitudes daily; and we know the possibilities that those who smile in our faces and want our votes may not have our best interests at heart. It's like that sweet white woman, Paula Deen. Despite her southern drawl, I would have never thought she would use racist, derogatory comments toward AMS. What is a political activist voter to do? Become apathetic? Not. Embrace the overcome, that is still down the road a piece.

Artistic expression has always prospered in the AMS community. Our community has followed lockstep with many cultural movements that have influenced us in words written, spoken, and sung. Our singers and rappers have represented those quirky advocates against the establishment that have rallied thousands and offended ten-thousands. They are truly no different from the poet Nikki Giovanni, the fighter Muhammad Ali, and the singer, James Brown. They express the acceptance of capitalism and its well-established belief system. These modern-day word rebels speak of hard-living in urban housing projects, frustrations with desiring unaffordable, material things, learning lessons from their living conditions, depending solely on a single mother; resorting to criminal behavior because of their living conditions, and expressing low self-esteem to the point of risking death to have more than a racist society wants to share.

Yet, our freed role in American society has never truly been defined. The AMS culture is one that has been directed into a niche of perpetual, subjugated development. Freed from slavery, we were given no direction on how to make the American system (education, capitalism, housing, farming, child-raising, etc.) work for us. When we tried, we were discouraged by lynching and riots.

We learned a desire for American success carried risks; a desire for a better education and a better place in society meant being brought to the attention of hate-mongers. In order to have some semblance of security, we lowered our thinking and expectations to concepts of mere survival; and America nullified in some regards and downgraded in others, an asset that has been at the core of what makes it great---the diverse thinking of its diverse people.

For security, psychological, physiological, and emotional, we assimilated into emulating the oppressor. Then, we assigned negative names to those who became successful imitators. From the confusion, we protested because no consistent standard had been established. From slavery's disunity we never gained unity; from ignorance we made great progress in education when segregated. Assimilation and integration revealed a country's desire while ongoing racism revealed a country's heart.

We married outside of our race and we loved everything and everybody that didn't remind us of a time when we were forced into a less-than-human status. Our Jewish brothers say never forget. The most powerful mechanism for the out of focus AMS community was the media and we used it well. Songs of uplifting spirits (religious and jazz) and songs of rhythm and blues that expressed our angst and desire began to prompt life to imitate art. And to this day, our youth imitate what the rapper protests.

But prioritizing the "renaissance" has come to a close. We

stagnate on old civil rights issues while homosexuals master the agenda and its accompanying methodologies. They fight with passion and commitment. We vacillate as a community because we only existed as one when our rights were openly suppressed. Now our purpose has been marginalized and we have bought into the melting pot theory without having community rituals and ceremonies to remind us of whom we were and who we are to represent. It is difficult to proclaim to my son that he has not gone through anything yet when he wants to rap and have a crisis to express. The crisis is continuous but his freedoms keep him from seeing it. That his grandfather would have been so much more and his father would have been so much more with a little financial direction, better employment, and opportunities that came from a few decades of teaching. That we could still be so much more but the struggle is so very much alive.

The Fourth of July

In 2012, as it will occur in oncoming Fourth of July holidays, AMS started making comments about our celebration of a day that represents a time in which AMS were enslaved. This has been a topic of discussion since the first celebration in America but due to the advent of social networks, one comment goes a long way.

Chris Rock (the comedian, remember, the comedian) made a comment about the holiday being a happy white folks day due to our enslavement at the time of the establishment of the holiday. This was nothing new for AMS because again, we actually let off a little steam with our talk. We still celebrate the day but we want everyone to know that we know what the real conditions were surrounding this holiday celebration of freedom/independence.

But in 2012, we find that making statements that are exclusive to "white folks" behavior often puts them on the defensive and they suffer "unrighteous indignation" over the revelation of historical misdeeds. Melissa Harris-Perry, author, professor, and host of her own news show, had the nerve to discuss the reality of the Fourth of July holiday; the fact that AMS were slaves on the day the holiday was originated. She was attacked by Bill O'Reilly and Gretchen Carlson. This is systemic and I understand more and more why the majority seeks to suppress or eradicate knowledge of their great sin. Now, black folks need to become revolutionaries in our position so that we can resist the efforts of those wannabe righteous and cleaners of past history.

In other words, we must become proactive in defending the truth. It may involve a little pain but sooner or later people will realize that you can't whitewash everything. Joe Williams made a sacrifice; Rick Sanchez made a sacrifice; and Melissa Harris-Perry felt a brief "Caucasian angst" for her truthfulness. She did an outstanding job of responding to her critics; and she even used statements by Chris Rock in her defense.

Of course, the Las Cruces Tea Party flew a Confederate flag on a float during a Fourth of July parade celebration; as a subtle reminder that independence for the country had more to do with honoring the white, slave-ridden south than slavery. They defended the action by saying "you can't change history."

The reference was to the fact that the Confederacy occupied New Mexico for a couple of weeks during the war. So, that's why they were flying the flag. I guess those two weeks mean more to them than fairness, consideration, and respect. Hmmmm? Of course that is nonsense but AMS who actually state real, meaningful, and culturally relevant history (that shouldn't offend anyone), hear statements to suggest that we should not bring that up.

The truth is that white folks who are proud of their ancestors Civil War experience have a right to bear some pride in the fact. But the war, for people who chose to separate from the union due to some nationalistic rebellion, should not be represented with flag-waving pride. So, honor the ancestor with a statue or with his name;

but the flag represents a time in this country that was not so honorable. The Confederate flag represents separatism and stubbornness at all cost; it represents racism. The message is racism when that flag is flown with pride.

Television Power

The following information has been supported with information from an article by Rebecca Wanzo, Huffington Post, Black Voices. "I Know You're Tired of Hearing About Girls, but How about a Puzzling Piece of History?" April 30, 2012.

In an effort to reveal her anguish caused by a new HBO television show, Ms. Wanzo reveals a brief history of AMS television shows and how they have been impacted by forces beyond their control; beyond the fact that good shows with consistent ratings, stay on television. The new HBO show apparently has a black female lead and her life lacks non-white folks.

It is totally amazing that Caucasian producers and writers can whitewash American television with impunity. Ms. Wanzo simply makes note that the community in which the black character lives, should "reflect the racial diversity of Brooklyn."

What a sincere, seemingly innocent request. Television programs don't bend over backwards to add a number of black characters to shows that don't share our cultural leanings. They may have one token character who has some different cultural ethnicity, and they should.

Not only are these television shows dismissing AMS from scripts but they are also dismissing us from places where we naturally appear in American culture. It's getting irritating to see television shows with all-white casts; in places where I know some black folks have to reside or work. So, not only are AMS actors missing in regular white environs (high society, white college roommates, buddies in a restaurant, etc.) but we are literally getting written out of places where America should expect to see us.

Ms. Wanzo writes that, "Most people have fairly racially homogenous social circles." She mentions that she, like many black folks, watched *Family Ties* and *Cheers* but we also watched "*The Cosby Show, A Different World, 227, Amen* and shows with black leads." AMS had television shows we could watch and talk about and all seemed well. Yet, in 2013, it appears, as Ms. Wanzo has stated, that we have moved backwards in the arena of black television. Thank you, Ms. Wanzo, for being that voice (I know there are a few others) crying out in the midst of the television wilderness.

I can remember when some crusader for minority rights tried to muscle the networks into creating more diverse programming. It took boldness and resolve and it was a just cause. The result was the addition of a Hispanic show to the television show rotation; and it was as if the powers that be snubbed their noses in the air and refused to be corrected.

I vaguely remember that diversity programs were supposed to be in place to ensure fair representation of minorities in television programming.   The   backlash   was   less   minority-television programming than ever; and this reveals the continued arrogance and disrespect shown by the mainstream against minorities; specifically, AMS.

As society sought to allow black folks to come into the mainstream, racial diversity apparently became a political, economic, and social goal. So, in the 1970's and 1980's, the AMS market was a growth market. Ms. Wanzo reveals that as networks began to struggle, "black shows seemed to be the go-to choice for networks." She provides some validation: "NBC was struggling before *The Cosby Show* became the lead show in its resurgence." FOX built up its network with "...*The Arsenio Hall Show, Martin, In Living Color, Living Single, Roc,*" and a drama with AMS as lead characters. The show was *New York Undercover*."

I remember these shows and they were fantastic. Everybody loved them and white folks were going around talking about them; and joking about the characters or seriously discussing elements of the plot.

I remember that American Soul knew to watch the black shows on the WB and UPN. I had an intense loyalty to these networks because of their efforts to include and sustain black programming. But the parent companies of the networks moved in a new direction, with some good white shows and suddenly the black people vanished. How do you go from profitable and filled with diversity to strictly white with less profitability? As in government, the racist agenda often precedes productivity and profitability goals. It doesn't make sense unless some higher ups have come together with a racist agenda. And there could be another reason that I would have never thought of but at the every-day Joe level, this smells like a conspiracy.

Clearly, the network was forced to deal with its identity associated with so much AMS programming; whether that had anything to do with the dropped networks or not. Could advertisers use such a "stigma" to reduce costs? Could it have caused problems with the network getting B-list actors for its shows? What's really scary is that thirty years ago, there were more black folks on television, on sitcoms, than there are today. Television had not been ordered to diversify; and society was not accustomed to diversity but the shows prospered. Talent is talent and racist bureaucracy is causing the nation to pay. What in the world will happen thirty years from now when everybody will be speaking Spanish?

Ms. Wanzo states that NBC is again having viewership issues in 2012 and it's reflecting in the ratings. Here we go again. Television no longer reflects the growing demographics and power among minorities. The executives are finding it difficult to change and I surmise that it has something to do with advertisers, who readily identify their markets. Sure, their dollars speak loudly but they cannot have the final say when it comes to diversification in television programming.

I'm not sure that it is the advertisers who can walk with their commercial dollars if they believe the programming is not conducive with their marketing strategies (i.e. appealing to white dollars since minorities have less to spend). The truth is AMS spends quite a lot of money on many product brands. Perhaps, the system will need some realignment or restructuring due to the larger, evolving, minority market.

Minorities will need to speed the process up by refusing to watch all-white casts in all-white shows. I have yet to understand how animated movies and futuristic movies have less and less minority characters when minorities are growing in America. I have learned how to be highly selective about what I watch on television; including commercials, comedies, old dramas, and new sci-fi shows. And I don't gravitate towards the white cast with one minority character thrown in as an after-thought. In these shows, you can almost forget that a minority character is in the script because he or she is rarely seen and has little impact on moving the plot forward.

Sports Power

Joe Williams
Friday, June 22, 2012

Joe Williams, a respected AMS reporter with an online political-based broadcasting company, made a mistake similar to that of Rick Sanchez: he spoke directly and succinctly about an observation regarding race in America and he used the term "white folks." Mr. Williams was making a comment about Mitt Romney, the Republican candidate for the 2012 election. He stated how comfortable Mr. Romney appears around people who are like him (white folks) and how "stiff and awkward" he appears in other venues (places absent of white folks.) Mr. Williams stated: "...he can't relate to people other than that. But when he comes on Fox & Friends, they're like him. They're white folks who are very much relaxed in their own company." My only critique of this statement would involve, why state the obvious. His comment was a bold statement into how liberal commentary can keep pace with the vitriolic, right-wing comments that are broadcasts over and over due to their volatile nature. The result was a proclamation that the mainstream will not allow liberals to make such comments. Hush Limbad and Sheik Hornity make comments daily that are borderline, if not blatantly, racist. The liberal media dances around it or they address it solely in the nature of civility. Oh, but let a Roland Martin, Rev. Sharpton, or Joe Williams make a statement regarding race and they get censored. And their statements are rather mild expressions of the truth; especially in comparison to conservative Republican radio hosts.

Power of Teamwork

Riddick Bowe in an article by Rick Maese (Washington Post Staff writer): "When the money go, they go. When the money left, whatever the case may be, all that stopped," he says. "Have a million friends. Once the money stop, the crowd goes away."

The vicious cycle continues as black athletes and media professionals are scrutinized about their money. We wonder who will end up broke, busted, and disgusted without establishing a system of protection, financial viability, and investment; based on the short span of time that the millions will flow. Riddick Bowe had to entrust his financial viability with a human being other than himself because he was not prepared to take care of his own money. Impulse control is a precious commodity when looking at the very brief periods of time when fame and fortune align.

Of course, people have to leave when the money leaves because you have taken care of their financial needs, no matter how inconsequential to you. They ate, partied, and had a roof over their heads with very little effort; and they were content with having no job because they had no need for money.

But absent the finances of a benefactor, these people have to take care of themselves. For survival's sake, they have to join the working stiffs of society; whereas the retired athlete may have a retirement or emergency account that reminds him or her that once it's gone, it's gone.

Many of our children take rap so seriously that they spend hours listening and honing their skills preparing for that fabled record deal. Many parents support them with sound equipment and time. But that deal is a contract that involves cost of studio time, marketing promotions, royalties, and distribution; and one-hit wonders that end their careers with nothing, abound.

Our famous iconic heroes become confirmations that we can't make it as a people; that we need special assistance because we can't handle money. But all we have ever needed is the expertise and honesty to learn about the system that was invented to make money with the artist's or athlete's talent. Often we hear of the manager who skipped town with the money or the manager made millions and is living lavishly while the former talent is penniless. The manager managed his or her money while taking a percentage of the talent's money for formulating appearances, contracts for record deals, and providing career direction. We hear of the accountant who took money when presented with the opportunity to keep records of great windfalls and expenses.

The important variable that should fuel the talent's management of funds is the fact that great amounts of money don't usually continue to fall upon anyone. Michael Jackson made huge amounts of money on some wildly successful albums then things slowed a bit. He reportedly continued spending as if those huge amounts of monies were still rolling in and how do you manage that? It is impulsivity and prideful avarice on a grand scale. You need someone whom you can trust to tell you the truth about your spending habits; and you need to have enough respect for the person to listen. Perhaps, all celebrities need to see a daily budget of how much money is on hand; how much is being spent a month; and how long it will take to have nothing left.

September 21, 2013

In 1988, Jimmy the Greek Snyder was an odds maker employed by CBS; he actually made predictions on NFL games and this served the needs of many gamblers across the world. He made the comment that black athletes had an unfair advantage when it came to jumping and running because our physical attributes were the result of being bred (during slavery) to produce a stronger person. He also made a comment about black employment in athletics. He stated: if AMS "take over coaching jobs, like everybody wants them to, there's not to be anything left for white people." His brutal honesty is to be appreciated twenty-five years later. Slave-breeding is an historical fact. And the former oppressor's insecurity about coaching jobs is obviously a historical and present-day fact. I disagreed with the firing and my opinion has never changed. It is good to know what is in the heart of those with whom you work and live; in order that we can at least have the opportunity to change hearts and minds and to compromise.

On September 20, 2013, Adrian Foster confessed that he received money in college. He appeared to have tired of the conversation that labeled college athletes as amateurs who should not receive pay for their work. He addressed his under-the-table money as if it was a small sum given to him in order to keep food in his refrigerator and to go out occasionally. Mr. Foster attempted to justify his confession with the castigation of college athletic administrators. He opined that six- and seven-figure salaries of NCAA and college administrators declared college athletics as professional. Mr. Foster spoke of participating in what was considered an amateur sport only in regards to the players and their status of not getting paid. But many people are making millions while college players get to trade brain and other physical injuries for tuition.

Adrian Foster probably will not be officially reprimanded or brought before any board because his truth is deeper than the risk of stirring up more truth like it. As of October 12, 2013, nothing has transpired regarding his confession.

Someone has to pay for this façade; this mirage of amateurism that allows a select group of white guys to make decisions for a sport that has a large amount of AMS athletes. And while they are at it, they can fix the situation in the NBA where ninety something The percent of the players are AMS and a about sixty-percent of the coaches are white. Let's deal with ownership issue later. But to be fair (remember, we AMS have an intense desire to be perceived as fair), our PTSD often prevents us from trying to be owners of anything. In the business of coaching, AMS coaches often have shorter tenures; a shorter timeframe to turn teams around. They also don't get to be a head coach again after being given one opportunity. Well, at least Ty Willingham received several chances to coach.

The NFL attempted to address the coaching diversity issue with the Rooney Rule, enacted in 2003 and named after the late Pittsburgh Steelers chairman, Dan Rooney. The rule simply states that every team must interview at least one minority candidate every time there is a coaching or general manager opening. In January 2013, of the 15 top vacancies in the NFL, none were filled by a minority. The two minority coaches and one general manager who lost their jobs, were not replaced by minorities and neither did they find new top job positions in the NFL. They were eight head coaching positions and seven general manager jobs.

I love the attempt to make things right in the NFL but the owners simply do an interview as an obligatory process to adhere to a nonbinding, inconsequential rule. I love the story about how Mike Tomlin, the young AMS coach of the Pittsburgh Steelers, was hired. He was interviewed as an obligation to the Rooney Rule and the organization suddenly realized that he was the best candidate for the job, and they hired him. Is it coincidental that the Steelers organization launched the coaching career of Tony Dungy who is responsible for hiring a number of AMS coaches who later became head coaches? As a Ravens fan, I almost hate the Steelers; but I love the way they run a football organization.

The social mores of owners and the lack of desire to train someone from scratch is definitely a roadblock to hiring minorities. But someone who had a desire to adhere to the rule and to the intent of the rule would venture into the ranks of Division II football coaches and the HBCUs to fill job openings. Of course transition or training programs would be in vogue and once given the experience these persons would qualify for these various openings; and more job vacancies would be filled by minorities.

If no other action is taken, these owners and the league needs to pay. Boycotts and request for stipulations in contracts should occur. By any means necessary, the players should ensure that change occurs now and not at some distant time in the future.

On Tuesday, April 8, 2014, University of Connecticut basketball star Shabazz Napier initiated one of the greatest movements in American history. NCAA basketball which has been modeled off the plantation system of management was faced with public ridicule from a collegiate star saying he went to bed hungry.

UConn's student-athlete handbook outlines provisions for food consumption and it says athletes can eat in any residence hall between the hours of 7 a.m. and 7:15 p.m; so, it makes sense that student-athletes with no access to snacks or transportation may frequently go to bed hungry.

On April 15, 2014, the NCAA council approved new rules that allowed student-athletes unlimited meals and snacks. The NCPA (National College Players Association) has begun a movement to unionize collegiate sports.

Donald Sterling is the owner of the NBA franchise Los Angeles Clippers; at least as of the day of this writing, April 27, 2014. He allegedly has been recently exposed on a tape revealing racist statements. I must say that I disagree with taping people secretly because most of us have said statements that we would be embarrassed by if the world knew what we really had going on in our minds. But this taping confirms an aspect of Mr. Sterling's personality that should have him being dismissed as an NBA owner/representative.

Although he is the owner of a team in a league with predominate minority representation; and he has a girlfriend who is apparently of a mixed, dark ethnicity, Mr. Sterling spoke about not wanting blacks to attend games with his girlfriend because it embarrasses him. If it is his voice on the tape, he specifically mentions to his girlfriend not to bring Magic Johnson to any games. Earvin "Magic" Johnson, a former superstar of the Lakers Showtime and now television commentator and basketball Goodwill Ambassador, has considered Mr. Sterling a friend.

It is the dilemma AMS faces in America. We are treated politely, as if we are friends when specific groups want something from us but we have to remember that those who treat us friendly are not necessarily our friends. Mr. Sterling received validation from Magic Johnson and the NACCP who was about to present him with a reward. This trivial validation based on his status as owner of a predominately AMS team and his gifts to the AMS community sort of hedged his bets on public image with the other side being a man who didn't want minorities living in apartment buildings that he owned. He said they smell; and Hispanics just sit on the porch all day...or something to that effect.

How does a racist, wealthy, old white man, garner the friendship of AMS notoriety and the support of an organization known for standing in the gap between racism and achievement in America? Magic was introduced to Mr. Sterling by the owner of the Lakers, the late Jerry Buss. Perhaps, Dr. Buss was trying to mend the racist heart of Mr. Sterling. It is easy to figure out how the NAACP got tricked: he gave them money. The money came in the form of free tickets provided for inner city children as an outreach of the NAACP.

Mr. Sterling is not a one-time offender. He has settled a lawsuit with the federal government for $2.7 million. In 2006, The U.S. Department of Justice sued Mr. Sterling for housing discrimination, claiming he refused to rent apartments to Asians and AMS, and families with children. The settlement was reached in 2009. He has also tendered racist remarks to former employees. Danny Manning was the brunt of racist remarks during a contract negotiation. Baron Davis and Elgin Baylor have also heard racist comments spew from the Clippers' owner.

The questions that arise with Donald Sterling's comments are not based solely on racism. Can a known racist owner, successfully operate a company filled with AMS employees in an AMS working environment, without hurting the entire corporate structure? Well, apparently he has done it up until now. I would like to say that there is no way it can continue to happen. Clipper-land has only recently become a place of relative success; and I think Mr. Sterling just returned the team to the gutters of the NBA with one stroke. On April 29, Adam Silver, the new league commissioner, banned Donald Sterling for life and immediately called for his termination of presence and interaction with basketball operations. The other owners have to vote on it.

What self-respecting AMS would want to go there to play for this self-proclaimed 'massa' and what player wants to renegotiate a contract with the team when 29 other teams can be propositioned about his services? An ESPN host, Bomani Jones brought this subject to light on a show when he discussed another aspect of the episode.

Mr. Jones brought up the fact that selective housing choices and white flight have combined to create the criminal environment in Chicago. The highways are built so that white folks who have left the city, can reenter for their good jobs without driving through neighborhoods of the disenfranchised. He further stated that people like Mr. Sterling have perpetuated this wrong by regulating where AMS can reside; and that Mr. Sterling's wife went around checking the ethnicity of the people who lived in their buildings by pretending to be a building inspector. And I thought she was so innocent in this whole thing. She asked Doc Rivers' (the coach) permission to watch the team in a playoff game. How sweet.

Donald Sterling's comments about blacks confirmed the debilitating role he plays in the detriment of AMS in the housing arena. But people knew... other owners knew the real Donald Sterling. They all knew. What is the issue with an elderly man concerned about his girlfriend spending public time with wealthy, virile, young brothers? I am not so old and not so rich and I would be concerned as well. Enough is enough. It may not be much Mr. Sterling but it looks as if you and your girlfriend helped to end this charade.

Even Bomani Jones couldn't do the entire situation justice. After all has been said and done, Mr. Sterling does not deserve to have his franchise snatched from under him based on one conversation and some lawsuits. I'm sorry but it's true on the most basic of business models. There have been many owners of businesses that employed AMS who were racists; and there still are some company presidents who have racists views as we so disappointingly found out about Paula Deen. She had such a sweet, Southern accent.

No, all things are not equal with Mr. Sterling mainly because he owns a company filled with uniquely talented individuals who play against teams of uniquely talented individuals; and most of them are AMS. All are employees but some actually shape the product which is the team and its media dollars. Lebron, Wade, Kobe, and Paul all help to define the product and I have a feeling that Mr. Sterling is done.

Whether the NBA had done something or not; they better had done something and they did. It is the power of the empowered AMS coming to the fore to provide an economic model that can change the world, starting with America. If Mr. Sterling remains as the owner, his investment will become worthless. Those employees are contracted business owners themselves and they will refuse to play for and against his team. He will lose and the racists will come out and support him and color will become extremely relevant in a business model that wants everyone to love each other so that all can get paid.

They don't want AMS players to flex their collective muscles because power like this is not taken lightly and can become addictive. Please, stay Mr. Sterling. We need a jumpstart to what is yet to come.

It has already started. The rumor is out that Lebron James will not step on the court next year (2015) if Donald Sterling is still in the league. I am excited. Again, please stay Mr. Sterling and see how God will use the most vilest of creatures, people, and situations to accomplish his just ends.

Cops and Robbing AMS

As I rode down the wide lanes of Liberty Road in Baltimore County in 1982, despite my years of drinking and smoking marijuana, I still had a semblance of the Christian principles that Handy and Lillie Stephens taught me. It was quite a treat for me to leave Florida and witness the AMS presence flooding the highways, running the businesses in the Woodmore community, and teaching in the schools. I almost felt compelled to turn the young AMS man in who gave me an outrageous deal on mirrored-tile for my new apartment.

I didn't have a clue about police brutality. Yes, I saw the water hoses and dogs turned on innocent African Americans on television---men, women, and children. I knew that government- sponsored abuse of my rights was a possibility and highly likely in my lifetime. But in my junior high school years, we demonstrated at my school (1973) and the police caught a man who was pulling guns from the trunk of his car. We were treated fairly and that was in central Florida; in Polk County. This was 1982, in the North (I thought), and I had experienced no police brutality in college in Tallahassee, Florida. I read about a college campus police officer who killed a man who coincidentally happened to be his estranged wife's lover. The man had been speeding in a car and the officer stopped him just at the edge of campus. The courtroom testimony informed the public that the officer had told the woman that he would kill the man and nothing would be done about it. Ironically, the people involved were all African Americans. I had known that cops had all sorts of unregulated authority on the street; and now I was learning that black police officers had such clout as well.

In Baltimore, I transported some teens who worked in my uncle's restaurant through Druid Park; although I didn't know that no traffic was allowed in the park at night. The youngsters had me take a shortcut. I was irate when the officer stopped me because I had done nothing wrong, I thought. The teens quickly informed me of my offense and I transferred my anger to them. They informed me that Baltimore cops routinely beat its citizens and it was best to be calm, polite and respectful.

Nothing prepared me for March 3, 1991. Rodney King had been subject to a traffic stop and he was surrounded by seven police officers. They beat him unmercifully; although a few of the officers just watched. For AMS, we knew that a miracle had happened in that a person had videotaped the beating because the world would have evidence that cops consistently brutalized members of our community. It didn't turn out that way. Four cops were tried and all were found not guilty; despite the evidence. South Central Los Angeles went ballistic and looted, burned, and caused mayhem.

A couple of days following the verdict, I was riding down Winands Road about a mile away from where I would move 15 years later. I drove into a speed trap. As the AMS officer prepared to write my ticket, some brothers in a car going the opposite direction yelled to him, "Let that man go. You saw what they did to Rodney King and they didn't do nothing. Let that man go."

And to my surprise, the officer gave no reply put merely closed his book and walked back to his car. I yelled thanks to the brothers and there was a strong sense of sticking it to the man despite the seeming insignificance of it all. It is this feeling that the majority race cannot comprehend. The frustration of being dealt with unjustly; and the occasional victory in which we refuse to be mainstreamed into an oppressive, unjust system that seems doggedly determined to disrespect us as if tradition demands it.

There is something about having authority to exercise brute force over other citizens. I was working at a retail giant of the 80's in the Assistant Management program. I had to manage a department and generally keep watch over the store with security. One day, a young, shabby-looking Hispanic gentleman stole some shoes. We followed him outside of the store and he began to run. We gave chase and finally caught him. As some of the guys held him, I could understand the core of his message. I made out a few of the Spanish words he was speaking. He was stealing the baby shoes for his daughter: "Los zapatos para mi nina...tres anos."

Initially, I felt the cultural angst of doing whatever it took to fulfill the most basic of needs. I felt empathy and no one else did. I told myself over and over again, crime is never the answer. As a newbie in management, I had to put on a good show and join in with my white brothers who were guardians of the right, without regards to personal plight. I should assimilate I thought. I should join in and care less about why he was stealing the $3 shoes; and I told myself he deserved his plight based on putting his life in the hands of these gung-ho white guys.

But they began to punch him, and punch him. And they asked if I wanted to get in a lick or two and it was totally beneath me to hit an unprotected man with six other guys around. I could not fathom anyone enjoying such a lowly activity as much as these guys; it seemed weak and immature and wicked to punch a guy who was apprehended and could not fight back.

Where is all the outrage? People think that those who do wrong lose their rights and I suspect the next jump would be to shoot people stealing purses or running away after cursing you and your family. I would think that AMS should request all AMS and minority cops to cross the blue line to ensure that this and other senseless police offenses do not go unpunished. Some bullies grow up and want to become cops. They pass the psychological evaluation and become weak, insecure, mentally unstable, faux tough-guys, with guns.

I commend those American Soul who became cops in the sixties. My uncle was one of them, a police officer in Washington, D. C. It was a time of upheaval in the country and many considered them sellouts. They took good jobs and they were needed to represent us in law enforcement. Just think about it. Every now and then you will find a Hispanic or American Soul in on the police brutality scene but think how many more cases of brutality there would be if no minorities were on the force.

The Officer Friendly program had police officers coming to our segregated schools and telling us that they were our friends. It was a comforting thought to think that local government had officers of the law looking out for the innocent citizens. But the reality was contradictory and cruel. We witnessed it, and we saw it on the news; cops turning water hoses and dogs on innocent citizens; and we knew of instances in which crimes were punished more harshly than usual because the criminal was American Soul. Unfortunately, we see in 2013 how brutality is still being carried out in the name of government institutions.

Too Much Sanford, Florida in America
April 6, 2007

Aaron Harrison was shot by police in a North Lawndale neighborhood in Chicago, as he zigzagged through an alley. He was shot in the back while being chased by police officers. The police officers stated that they were in fear for their lives as they ordered Aaron to drop the gun and he refused. A lawsuit was filed and the lawyer revealed how the police officers' version of the incident was implausible. Late Thursday afternoon, August 15, 2013, Aaron Harrison's mother was awarded a settlement of $8.5 million. The money could not make up for the loss of a son and it could not make up for the loss of another young member of our community.

There were four witnesses who said that there was no gun present when the young 18-year old was shot. Some common threads appear when AMS are shot down on the streets. Either a car used as a weapon or a fictitious gun are often cited as reasons why the young men are killed. I wonder how many stories are there of white guys getting shot in the back during a police chase or having a gun when no gun is found? No charges have been brought against the officer who shot Aaron. The punitive damages have increased the $54 million in settlements in the city due to police misconduct.

Now here's reality. In 1999, Amadou Diallo was killed while reaching for his wallet. Three of the five detectives involved in the hail of bullets pumped into Mr. Diallo went to trial and were found not guilty. They said that the victim gestured with his hands and they thought he was reaching for a gun. AMS are caught between a rock and a hard place when it comes to addressing local law enforcement that has represented racist authority against local residents in communities throughout America.

Even obeying the law can get AMS killed. Some young men were compliant with police authority; one rose up from the ground in his own driveway; and one sought to protect himself. They all were shot and/or killed. When cops make a mistake, they are trained to contain the situation by limiting the number of witnesses; so while the hail of bullets (over 40) sent at Mr. Diallo may seem too extreme to the average citizen, they serve a practical purpose in denying the public the opportunity to hear the victim's side of the story. Hence, George Zimmerman's version of the story was heard and not Trayvon Martin's.

It was November 25, 2006.

A young man named Sean Bell and two friends (Joseph Guzman and Trent Benefield) were out partying because he was soon to get married. It was his bachelor party and it was being conducted at Club Kalua, a strip club in Jamaica, Queens in New York. Sean Bell was getting married that day; this was the morning before his wedding and excitement was in the air. Perhaps he should have chosen a different way to celebrate but he didn't deserve to die because of the place he chose to be entertained. It was to be his "last hurrah" prior to settling into the stability and comfort of marriage.

He was of the legal age having been born May 19, 1983. His fiancée, Nicole Paultre, had birthed a daughter by him and their marriage was sure to have a great deal of meaning for them.

The owners of the club were under investigation for promoting prostitution (What, not in a strip club!?); so, several undercover officers were all about the club. Officer Isnora stated that he heard someone say, "Get my gun," so he followed a young man out to his car. Here it gets iffy but everything that could go wrong, went wrong. A man is seen walking up to the car with a gun drawn; but it's the police; who knew? Young men in the car had to panic as would most of us. The driver, Sean Bell, starts driving off and brushes his would-be assailant's leg, who happens to be an undercover cop, Officer Isnora. Yet, if Officer Isnora followed them to check if someone in the group was going to get a gun, shouldn't he have been satisfied and got out of the way when the men were obviously driving away? Statements were released concerning whether Officer Isnora identified himself as a cop. He actually pinned his police badge on to the outer parts of his jacket to identify himself. I am sure no one was looking for that in the angst and excitement of the moment. But, up until this moment, no crime has been committed according to the standards established by America's judicial system. Even brushing the leg with a car means that you have lived and no one has threatened anyone.

Officer Isnora shot into the vehicle 11 times; and Officer Michael Carey shot three times. Sean Bell was shot four times in the neck.

Had it been three or four Caucasian males riding in the vehicle, surely they would not have been perceived as a threat---no matter how close the vehicle came to running over the officer.

On July 28, 2010, the city of New York reached an agreement with Nicole Paultre Bell for $3.25 million dollars. Bell's friend, J. Guzman will receive $3 million. Trent Benefield, the other friend, collects $900,000. The cops had been acquitted of criminal charges in 2008 and the Justice Department dismissed civil rights claims. Sean Bell has streets named after him and flowers laid on his grave but he is dead...and his wife and family can only imagine another life that has been snatched away by the systematic oppression of AMS by police officers.

A young man named Oscar Grant III was shot on New Year's 2010 and a short video was taken of the incident. It was shown all across the country as an Oakland transit cop stood over a subdued, immobilized Oscar Grant, and fired a single shot into his back while fellow officers watched. The officer was convicted of involuntary manslaughter instead of murder; and as with any police officer, one would think it to be difficult to prove that he intended to murder any suspect.

A movie was made of this incident starring, Michael B. Jordan (Red Tails, Pastor Brown), called Fruitvale Station.

On January 30, 2010, people packed the courthouse to hear the involuntary manslaughter conviction of BART (Bay Area Rapid Transit) police officer Johannes Mehserle. Some of those people in the courtroom were family members and friends of the victim. Many were people who most assuredly had crimes committed against them or a history of crimes committed against friends and family members. This trial was a testament to the cliché that the more things change, the more they stay the same. For a man to stand over a human being, with his finger on the trigger, and shoot another human being in the back, is a disgrace to those who wear law enforcement uniforms with honor. To shoot a man in the back who is not even a threat while lying on the ground, should require years in jail and continued psychological evaluations.

So, 674 days after Mr. Grant's murder, Los Angeles Superior Court Judge Robert Perry imposed the disrespectful and offensive sentence of 24 months of incarceration, with credit for time served of 292 days. Michael Vick received 24 months for killing dogs. But just in case I'm being too judgmental as we AMS can be in dealing with the oppressive majority and the justice system, let's reflect upon some rational issues. One, Mr. Mehserle had a serious lapse in judgment; but whether in anger or poor training, he took a life. Two, whatever the crime Mr. Grant may have committed, execution was neither the punishment nor to be carried out without trial by jury. Three, any judge with respect for the people (all people) would take in consideration the nature of the poor decision that caused Mr. Grant's death and orphaned his children. A white woman killed her husband who was a minister and claimed abuse after the fact. There had been no hint of abuse but the judge still sentenced the woman to six years. Mr. Mehserle stood over Mr. Grant while the demons yelled, "Go ahead; do him!" Surely, in the heart of darkness, an angel had to yell "whatever you do, don't pull the trigger." But he pulled the trigger anyway.

He had time to think and reflect upon the consequences of capturing Mr. Grant while in the midst of the chase, and he had time to think about it prior to pulling the trigger. The judge had time to think about it; and obviously he wanted to send a message: that black lives are only equal to the precious lives of dogs.

The movie "Fruitvale Station," depicts the many sides of Oscar Grant as it seeks to humanize AMS...criminals and average citizens. Mr. Grant was not shown as a perfect person. He had some good qualities but he was also engaged in criminal activities; and he was a former convicted felon, and a drug dealer. He was 22 years old, a great father, and a loving son. Mr. Grant didn't deserve to die after being captured by local law enforcement.

December 31, 2010

Bobby Tolan is a former professional baseball player who spent 15 years in the league. At first glance, it had to appear to be a good decision to live in Bellaire, Texas. It was a good community, and predominantly white so the chances of trouble finding his son by association was slim. Bobby had been a successful athlete and he had the right to live wherever he could afford; to meet his standards and specific requirements for his family.

But the country doesn't work like that . at one time, bankers, principals, and mine workers lived in close-knit communities because AMS with money were still AMS and forced to live among their own folks. But in late December 2008, surely enough change had taken place that wealthy AMS could live wherever they wanted to live, in Texas as well.

Robert Tolan and his cousin, Anthony Cooper, pulled the family Nissan SUV into their driveway after stopping at a burger joint, at around 2am. Unbeknownst to them, police officers had followed them as suspects in the theft of a car that had not been reported stolen (yeah, you figure it out). Twelve cars had been stolen from the wealthy community and I am sure it was a priority to find the culprits who were doing it. Being outstanding police officers, they stopped the teens to check out the likelihood (since they were black) of them driving an unreported stolen car...um?

To Officer Jeffrey Cotton's credit, his partner, Officer John Edwards apparently typed in one digit wrong and the vehicle came back on the computer as stolen. That's a strange coincidence that the one-digit mistake turned up a stolen car that looked like the SUV the young Tolan was driving.

Officer Edwards ordered the young men out of the car, with his weapon drawn. He called for backup. While the guys were on the ground, I can imagine their righteous indignation at being stopped as law-abiding citizens, and being told to get on the ground in their good clothes, in Robbie Tolan's own driveway. They probably quickly realized that this was one of those crimes that they had heard about but never experienced: DWB, driving while black. The young men should have been safe in their own driveway, and as American citizens they deserved polite consideration; especially, since they weren't resisting arrest or making unreasonable jabs at the officers.

At the very least, one of the officers should have informed some civilian (the owners of the property) regarding their stop and persistent presence in the family's driveway. Were the computers working that identified the car tags with the home? Perhaps they didn't think about that or perhaps the program doesn't match the owner's address. Ok. They couldn't pull up that information. How about the audio-visual of a protective mother and father emerging from the house to see what was happening, and to render verbal clarity? Good thing for caring, dignified mothers, you would think.

Mom and Dad shed more light on the situation, and provided order as they told the young men to shut up and lie down as the officer had instructed. Well, thank God for mothers. She provided a less threatening (I would hope) image that was providing additional information for children and adults alike. But apparently the cop did not want to hear it and neither did he allow her comments to diffuse the situation. She stated that the men on the ground were her sons and the car that the officer yelled about and pulled his gun about was not stolen. Case over, let's go home, Dirty Harry; live to shoot an AMS another day.

Instead, the cop apparently got aggressive enough towards the mother, Marian, that the young man felt a need to come to her assistance. Officer Jeffrey Cotton had grabbed Mrs. Marian Tolan by the arm and positioned her towards the house. Young Robert lifted himself from the ground, yelled an expletive regarding touching his mother, and for that defiance, he was welcomed with a bullet in his chest.

From the police officers stopping at the house, to the shooting, took less than one minute. Yes, a real live round fired by a white police officer on an unarmed AMS lying in his own driveway. The 'trespasser' police officer fired a bullet that punctured the young

Tolan's lung and lodged in his liver. It seems as if the officer made a mistake but decided to save face by antagonizing enough people to the point that he would be forced to (or take advantage of an opportunity) shoot someone. Sounds like George Zimmerman creating an opportunity to kill where none should have existed.

Who can pay for the lack of respect generated by government and law enforcement for generations? It should not be the people. There is a cultural gap of insensitivity that AMS has to always know of lest we slip and dash our heads against the stones of murderous hypocrisy.

For the Tolans, it reeks of racial profiling and discrimination. They lived in a really nice community; and had a really nice car, I assume. And in such nice communities, no matter how many 'good' AMS live in them; the good people (the majority folks) must watch out for those of dark hue. If I live on the other side of the community, I may know that there are two families of AMS living in my community but I probably will never meet them. For police officers, it gets even more harried. They don't live in the community and they get to ride around late at night and gently profile the neighborhood; like George Zimmerman. I'm sure that they think profiling helps to reduce the time spent on watching innocent white folks. Even if Officer Cotton thought it was a stolen vehicle, he should have yelled *"my bad* ...that's my mistake for the stop." Then he should have pretended to get a call, turned on the siren, and got the heck out of those people's driveway; especially when the owner came out of the house and identified her sons and their car. Someone needs to pay for this, other than the Tolan family.

April 10, 2012

Officer Jeffrey Cotton had been charged with aggravated assault in the December 31, 2008 crime. On May 11, 2010, the Tolan family released a statement regarding their disappointment in the 'not guilty' verdict. Recent updates to this article were obtained from an article by Janet Shan, the Hinterland Gazette, April 10, 2012 (Houston Police Dodge Lawsuit Over Shooting of Black Man Robert Tolan in Case of Mistaken Identity). A federal judge ruled that the officers have immunity against claims in the shooting due to the officer fearing for his life. So, a jury trial found Officer Cotton to be within his rights as a police officer to attempt to kill a young black man in his own driveway (my God) and a federal judge says the family can't sue for damages.

Robbie will have to forgo his athletic dreams as the bullet lodged inside of him will impact his life and career; a double whammy. Proud parents, Marian and Bobby, will now focus on something else to be proud of about their son and they will make it. Bobby probably saw a lot of discrimination when he came along in major league baseball. But he made it; only to have it lurch over his life and his family, until it came down and roosted in his driveway; cock-a-doodled with its head in the air, and mysteriously laid an egg. Like AMS all over this country, he may have Post Traumatic Stress Syndrome; and most of us qualify for that.

How Can We Nurture a New Generation When the Best and Brightest Are Struck Down BY THE OLD THAT WON'T CHANGE AND WON'T DIE?

In Pleasantville, New York, a nice community, a police officer shot and killed a 20-year-old college football player/student for Pace University, On October 17, 2010. The circumstances of the shooting are highly questionable. The murder occurred outside of a bar in Thornwood, N.Y. as the late Mr. DJ Henry was sitting in his Nissan Altima with two friends.

A police officer, Ronald Gagnon, approached the car and motioned for the young man to pull away from a fire lane. As the student moved forward, apparently, Henry, Jr. drove away in the path of another officer, Aaron Hess. Officer Hess jumped in front of the car and ordered it to stop prior to shooting the student. Witnesses say that Danroy Henry, Jr. was driving away.

The police report states that the boy attempted to run the police officer down with the car. Hmm? This seems easy to prove or disprove. Mr. Hess waged war on an unarmed citizen and shot through the windshield. Another officer also fired into the vehicle and DJ Henry was killed. Another passenger, Brandon Cox, was shot in the arm. Why would the student attempt to run over a police officer; unless he nervously over-reacted when told to move out of the fire lane (many of us avoid conflict with cops) and he accidentally pulled out too fast and almost struck the cop? What was so life-threatening that you had to get on the hood of the vehicle and pull the trigger?

Of course, in a bad shooting, the police dashboard cameras are conspicuously turned off or inoperable. Another police officer's camera caught the chaos after the shooting. Six months after the shooting, the Police Benevolent Association of the Pleasantville Police Department gave Officer Aaron Hess the Police Officer of the Year award while an investigation was still underway about whether or not he unjustly took this young man's life. Mr. Henry, Sr. said it well concerning the award: "That is in keeping with the arrogance displayed and the inhumanity that we have seen from that moment he was killed." The dilemma is whether or not this story should go under Crooked Cops. The verdict is still out.

March 12, 2012

The officer Aaron Hess was found not guilty of wrongdoing. The parents of Danroy Henry, Jr. plan to sue the officer.

March 7, 2012

Wendell Allen, another 20-year old AMS happened to be home where five children were in the home. A marijuana raid occurred and Mr. Allen surprised New Orleans Police Department officer Joshua Cloclough. He appeared at the top of the stairs in his home, descending towards the officer who shot him once in the chest, killing the son of Natasha Allen.

Officer Cloclough refused a deal that would have charged him with negligent homicide. He would have served less time than the four years he was given after pleading guilty to manslaughter. The officer apologized to the family and life goes on except for the priceless resource lost in the form of the potentially-great, Wendell Allen.

June 5, 2010

In Baltimore, a police officer, Gahiji A. Tshamba, shot and killed another man outside of a bar due to a confrontation over a woman. Apparently, Tyrone Brown, 32-years of age and a former marine, made the fatal mistake of groping the buttocks of the off-duty officer's date. There was a confrontation but Mr. Brown wasn't armed. Officer Tshamba, a 15-year police veteran, fired 13 times from his authorized Glock handgun and struck the victim six times. Apparently, alcohol and guns really don't mix (duh); even if you are an officer of the law.

It is pervasive; the taking of lives of inner city AMS with random ease and little regrets. On August 16, 2011, Officer Tshamba was sentenced to 15 years in prison.

November 19, 2011

There are so many stories that it hurts to leave one out. The death of the former retired Marine, Kenneth Chamberlain, Sr. is a fatality that epitomizes the hurt, pain, and precautionary measures that many people in our communities take and we still get slaughtered.

Mr. Chamberlain fought for his country and retired. He also worked for 20 years with the Westchester County Department of Corrections. This brother utilized a commonly known strategy of minorities for escaping classism in America---join the military. And after serving your country faithfully, take advantage of the various benefits offered to military veterans; including favorable consideration for government jobs, especially those involving security or prison guards.

To top it all off, Mr. Chamberlain had reached the ripe old age of 68 and at this age, the AMS community usually assumes that we are beyond the years of mistaken identity and police brutality. Apparently, this is not a factor in White Plains, New York.

The details are sickening. The late Mr. Chamberlain wore a medical alert bracelet due to a heart problem and apparently it was triggered in error. It alerted the customer service of the company that monitored his device; and the emergency medical technicians and the police, were called. Of course, a cautious, leery Mr. Chamberlain refused to open his door. He had no emergency and he informed his 5am visitors of such.

Unfortunately, he lived in public housing and no one took his word that he was alright. Instead, the police officers tried to break into his home to ensure that he was doing fine. He asked them to leave but these cops were so enthusiastic about saving him that they ignored his pleas to just leave him alone. The medical alert system recorded all of the unkind words yelled at this senior American citizen, former Marine, who just wanted to be left alone.

One of the cops who so wanted to help the AMS citizen called him the N-word. Once inside, the cops tased him, shot him with a bean bag gun, and oddly decided to shot him with real bullets...this elderly man who said he needed no help and had not broken the law outside of his home. They forcibly entered his home to help him and ended up taking Mr. Chamberlain's life. Of course, they say that he came at them with a butcher knife and they feared for their lives I assume. Blah, blah, blah...the man is dead.

Of course, the grand jury decided no criminal charges would be filed and a civil law suit has been initiated by the son of the victim.

If you put yourself in the cops' shoes, wouldn't you think about the possible ramifications of forcibly entering a man's home and killing him? Yes, you would if he lived in the beautiful single family homes of White Plains or in the mansions; but some cops think of AMS as less than a citizen based on where they live. And they kill us based on the color of our skin; realizing that nothing will happen to them as long as they kill us one by one in different parts of the country.

Give Up Some Ground, Florida!

February 26, 2012

On the night of February 26, 2012, teenager Trayvon Martin was shot dead by an overzealous, self-proclaimed, neighborhood watch captain, George Zimmerman. 911 calls reveal that Mr. Zimmerman noticed the young black teen and declared him to be suspicious although he was doing nothing suspicious other than returning from the store. It was a gated community and he was staying with his father; I can assume that Mr. Zimmerman had never seen the boy in the community.

But surely, in a gated community the consideration could have been given that the boy was allowed in the community and he was living somewhere within the gates. The unofficial watch captain stated that the young teen "looked suspicious." Apparently this was nothing as he then stated that the boy took off running. Mr. Zimmerman was heard mumbling to himself that these guys "always get away." The 911 operator made it clear that he was not to follow the potential suspect...the suspect called a suspect only because he was walking while black. Later, a recording sounded as if he made reference to "f...ing coon..." but this was not substantiated. Mind you, nothing has been stated by Mr. Zimmerman as to say from what the boy is escaping or getting away.

The most shocking thing is that several people called 911 and the tapes also reveal that the boy was shouting for help over and over; until a gunshot and the cries for help stopped. Later, his defense attorney made it an issue that the cries for help came from Mr. Zimmerman; although it is unlikely for a man to yell "help" when he has a gun, and is prepared to use it. If anything, the man with the gun would warn the person he was about to shoot, saying something like: If you don't get your black hands off me I'm going to SHOOT YOU DEAD.

And to make matters worse for the unofficial, disobedient watch captain, young Trayvon was talking to his girlfriend about some guy following him and that he was trying to get away. The young lady heard Zimmerman question Trayvon and then there was a scuffle. Instead of dealing with this fact, the defense questioned the veracity of the teenage witness's testimony; largely based on her cultural interaction (seemingly standoffish, angry, and oddly stubborn) when asked questions by legal authorities.

It is how a great deal of AMS women conduct themselves under the questioning of authoritative figures. The cultural misunderstanding probably biased the jurors against perceiving the core issue of a man killing a teen with literally no cause. But, it shouldn't have mattered.

How does a man attack a child and shoot him and not get charged until 44 days later and several nationwide protests? Mr. Zimmerman was not charged initially (he has a permit for the weapon) and supposedly it was due to his squeaky clean record; and some odd law in Florida (Stand Your Ground) that gives one the right to defend yourself with deadly force if you feel threatened. If you feel threatened? Uh-uh. White folks and some AMS alike may feel threatened when walking down the street and a hooded brother crosses the street to approach them. He may have only wanted directions but this night he gets killed?

Interesting law, but how does it apply when you initiated the threat? The defense did not use the law. But if you have an enemy that you want to kill legally, just take a gun and go to their house and get into an argument...then BAM! Just make sure that you are in Florida or one of the other states that have the "Stand Your Ground" law.

I am a native Floridian from central Florida and the cops have not been too friendly over the years. Turns out, Mr. Zimmerman had been charged in 2005 with resisting arrests with violence and battery on a law enforcement officer. Zimmerman had been the source of earlier complaints by the residents of the gated community and an emergency meeting had been called to address his tactics. One resident had complained about the watch captain approaching him and also coming to his home. Zimmerman's father wrote a letter to the press stating that he was a minority (white Hispanic) as well; and got along with AMS. I don't like when Caucasians mention working with or eating with, or being friends with black folks as a reasonable defense to their personal affront against AMS. The issue is that racial profiling apparently led to the demise of an innocent teen.

It took 44 days for him to be charged with second-degree murder. With a few well-placed lies, George Z.'s defense only has to create a reasonable doubt. It would have been better (in my opinion) to charge him with manslaughter. Basically, murder requires the defense to prove that George Zimmerman planned on killing Trayvon Martin. He may have but there is no way of proving it and surely the state attorney's office had to know this. Manslaughter says you killed someone with no intention to do it; you started out doing something that resulted in a death. Clearly, manslaughter was the way to go. But it's Florida...they could have never charged him and AMS (Negroes, Colored folks, Blacks, African Americans) would have had to deal with it.

You have to be thankful for Pastor Jamal Harrison-Bryant (Baltimore) and other AMS leaders traveling to the community and addressing the issue as a national topic. Hopefully, such horrific issues will lessen as more of the establishment realizes that we are sick and tired of our youth being targeted by villains of all hues.

On Friday, May 18, 2012, photos of George Zimmerman's bleeding head wound and his personal physician's statement that he suffered a possible broken nose were released. A statement that Trayvon had marijuana in his blood was also released. We can infer that this release of information was some oddball attempt to legitimize the taking of Trayvon's life. If a person had heroin in their blood along with being legally drunk, no one has the right to murder him or her.

On July 6, 2013, the prosecutors rested their case in the trial of George Zimmerman. The trial lasted from June 10-July 13, 2013. The issue of who cried out became a major issue because of the second-degree murder charge. If it was George Zimmerman, it creates the doubt needed to say he didn't really want to kill Trayvon. Again, why would a man with a weapon, ready to shoot, cry out, "Help me, help me!" when he is obviously ready to defend himself with extreme prejudice? Trayvon Martin would still be alive had George Zimmerman been obedient to the police dispatcher's statement/warning for him not to follow the young teen. Mr. Zimmerman would have never been on trial for murder had he done what the dispatcher told him to do.

July 13, 2013

This evening at a little pass 10pm, the six-woman jury with one minority, found George Zimmerman not guilty of all charges; including manslaughter. My mind flashed to water hosing AMS against buildings; putting our heads down as we walked by white folks; and black guys getting charged with rape when a white girl decided she loved a brother. Angela Corey appeared giddy as she held a press conference after the verdict. I became paranoid as if this was another one of those great conspiracies designed to degrade and demoralize AMS.

What if the state prosecutor's office knew that a second-degree murder charge was reaching too high and that Mr. Zimmerman would get off because you could not prove his guilt beyond a reasonable doubt? What if they prosecuted merely to appease public pressure because after 44 days, evidence had to be skewed, faulty, or insufficient; ensuring that George Zimmerman could not be tried fairly?

In the wake of national attention, the state decided to prosecute. The state had to go through the motions of prosecuting, knowing that reasonable doubt would prevail. What if Angela Corey, on the night of Zimmerman's acquittal, experienced the euphoria of having done her job and dodged a bullet simultaneously. After 16 hours of deliberation and 13 hours on Saturday the jurors freed Zimmerman; a man who has to live with the fact that he obviously initiated an altercation which resulted in his killing an unarmed AMS teen.

The President finally came out with a definitive statement regarding the verdict. He explained the anguish of injustices felt by AMS over generations. He expressed our experiences with being treated like second-class citizens. And amazingly, some white folks were angry.

We are receiving our pay for assimilating; for following a narrowed, deliberate, sparsely adorned path provided by the former oppressor. We need to understand that we have all paid enough; enough is enough.

Stand Your Ground was played out some years earlier, with some role reversals. In the year 2010, Trevor Dooley walked across the street from his home, after yelling to stop kids from skateboarding in a neighborhood park. He came a little closer and yelled, and David James, an Iraq War Veteran, answered back in defense of the kids. Mr. James stated that there was no sign to say that the kids could not skateboard. He had his 8-year-old daughter with him. As fate dealt the hand, the players were Trevor Dooley, a 69-year-old AMS bus driver and David James, a 41-year-old Caucasian man.

The older man came over to chase the kids away and the younger man stood up in defense of the kids. The verbal disagreement between the two turned into a physical altercation with the younger man using his strength to subdue the older man.

The daughter of David James testified that the older Dooley tried to walk away but her dad kept him from leaving.

"Yeah, like my dad got on top of him to keep him down," the girl testified.

The black man fired a single shot and killed the white man. As in the Martin case, the unarmed person was killed by the armed person who claimed that he feared for his life. How long did the 69-year-old black man walk around free before he was arrested? George Zimmerman walked around for 44 days prior to his arrest. Mr. Dooley was arrested in less than two days and charged with manslaughter, despite the "stand your ground" law. In the Trayvon Martin murder, the people marched and protested; and it took 44 days before something was done.

It is the uneven application of American justice that is designed to keep us humbled and humiliated. We see it and hear it until we don't expect fairness in any system (social, governmental, employment, etc.). At least, that's what the continued misapplication of justice in our communities is supposed to do.

Anne Coulter, right-wing conservative and author, weighed in on the controversy by comparing critics of Zimmerman to the KKK, on, of all places, "The Laura Ingraham Radio Show." Huh? Ms. Ingraham is the lady who called one of her devoted listeners a racial epitaph, over and over again. Her listener was married to a Caucasian man and was displeased with the treatment she received from her in-laws.

Laura Ingraham decided to go Torah on the sister, "...so shall I add tenfold thereto."Ms. Coulter defended the freedom of Mr. Zimmerman by saying that not everything goes to trial. As intelligent a woman as she believes herself to be, she always criticizes the minority viewpoint; while supporting the viewpoint that favors Caucasians.

In other words, Caucasians can do no wrong in her eyes and all perspectives are tainted with her personal, racial bias. With a perspective such as hers, she has to be placed in the media, with a station, that represents the Caucasian point of view. Fair, unbiased news reporting is not their jobs; so, who wants them on television? It is fair to say that their main support comes from racists white folks or people who don't relate to AMS culture. So, who advertises on this station during her show? Let's find out and do something about it.

Whoa! Just saw the advertisement. Apparently, she's doing a political show with George Stephanopoulos on CBS. This stinking systemic racism is all around us so where do we begin? The answer is one area and one step at a time; but we have to take the initial steps.

November 23, 2012

George Zimmerman is waiting to be tried. But a new "Stand Your Ground" challenge has emerged and another AMS Florida teen is dead. Michael Dunn, a 45-year-old white guy, thought it his civic duty to tell four young black guys in an SUV that their music was too loud, while he pulled up alongside in his vehicle at a service station. I suspect that there may have been a plan on shooting the young guys because I would never pull alongside young brothers with loud music let alone tell them to turn it down. I would have gone to another pump, but not Michael Dunn.

He felt threatened with the potential response. Hmm. A white guy telling four brothers in an SUV to lower their music...he should have felt threatened. He imagined seeing a shotgun peeping through the window; imagined since none was found and his girlfriend didn't see it. Mr. Dunn readily fired upon the young guys. Three bullets struck Jordan Davis, taking his life far too early like so many other young black men. Dunn was charged with first degree murder and three counts of attempted murder. The "Stand Your Ground" law appears to work well when white guys take a notion to killing black men but it appears less prosecutable when a black man kills a white guy under more threateningly real circumstances. So, here we are in 2012 with another legal conspiracy seemingly aimed at the destruction of black folks.

May 23, 2013

The attorneys representing Mr. Dunn accused the Duval county judge, Suzanne Bass of misconduct; and she agreed to step down. Judge Mallory Cooper was appointed to handle the trial in May and as of July 2, 2013, she has been replaced by Judge Russell Healey. I would like to think that this would be an ideal opportunity for the state of Florida to partially redeem itself with a speedy trial, with a reasonable reflection of ethnicities on the jury box, and a verdict that corresponds to the evidence. No gun was found at the scene and Mr. Dunn fled after shooting the teen.

On February 17, 2014, Michael Dunn was convicted of three counts of attempted murder (one for each of the living teenagers in the vehicle) but it was a hung jury on the charge of murder of young AMS 17-year old Jordan Davis. Mr. Dunn faces a minimum of 60 years in prison for the convictions. A hung jury usually leaves the prosecution with the option of a retrial, making a deal, or dropping the charges. Since this is the beautiful but controversial state of Florida (controversial when it comes to AMS issues), a good prosecutorial recommendation would be to avoid a retrial because it's so crazy down there that Mr. Dunn may just get away with everything. Of course, that's not possible; or is it only possible in Florida?

Mr. Dunn has been scheduled for a retrial in September 2014 for the murder of Jordan Davis.

It is things like the case of Marissa Alexander that keep us skeptical and aware about the consequences of advocating for every incident that comes along. Marissa is an AMS woman who supposedly stood her ground and shot a warning shot at her physically abusive husband; now, she is serving time and has been subjected to the "10-20-life" rule in Florida (yes, my home state of Florida, again). It is a mandatory sentencing guideline regarding the use of a firearm in the commission of a felony. Producing a firearm in commission of a felony requires a minimum 10-year sentence. Firing a firearm requires a minimum 20-year sentence. (Some information excerpted from article on Love My Black.com, posted April 17, 2012). Again, this is in my home state of Florida; Jacksonville, Florida. I always thought the justice system in northern Florida, Duval County, behaved a little better than their central Florida counterparts and perhaps I am correct.

Marissa Alexander had a permit to carry a weapon. Allegedly , she needed it as her second husband allegedly had a history of domestic violence against Marissa and documented abuse against women. Not so. He had been arrested on a domestic violence charge involving his brother and those charges were dropped. On September 30, 2009 an injunction had been issued against Mr. Gray. She placed an injunction against her husband that was in effect on the evening of August 1, 2010. Mr. Rico Gray states that he never hit a woman in his life. Mr. Gray states that she wrote a letter and visited the Florida District Attorney to reveal that she had lied on her husband; and the restraining order was modified so that they could be around each other without violence.

Eventually, she had a restraining order placed on her because she was physically abusing Mr. Gray; and continued to do so while she was out on bail awaiting trial for aggravated assault. She gave Mr. Gray a bloody, swollen eye. Sounds like Marissa may have anger management issues.

Mr. Rico Gray and Marissa Alexander shared a home as husband and wife. She kept the last name of her ex-husband and had a daughter with him. They apparently had been having marital difficulties as Marissa had frequently spent the night outside of the house. She returned on the night of August 1, 2010. Mr. Gray and his sons returned to the house later and did not know that she was inside the house. Marissa parked her truck in the garage. Remember that fact.

He allegedly attacked her in a jealous rage (saying the baby delivered by Marissa days earlier was not his child); while she was using the bathroom. Mr. Rico Gray states that his had pictures of their newborn baby on her phone and offered him a chance to look at the pictures while she went to the bathroom. According to Mr. Gray, as Marissa went to the bathroom he went through her text messages and discovered a number of texts to her ex-husband. He went to the restroom and asked her about the text messages and Marissa grew angry about him looking through her phone messages.

Mr. Gray says he turned and stated, "I'm outta here!" He told his two boys to get their things because they were leaving. At the time of this violent altercation, his sons were ages 9 and 12. They were Marissa's step-sons. The story goes that he shoved her, strangled her, and prevented her from leaving his presence. Supposedly, she temporarily escaped and retrieved her weapon in the garage but she was unable to leave through the garage.

Mr. Gray states that Marissa came out of the bathroom and began hitting him as she had done in the past when she was angry. When he said he was leaving, she went to the garage to get her gun and returned to the living room area where she fired a shot above the head of Mr. Gray and his sons. They ran a number of houses down the road and called 911. Eventually, SWAT came to the house and she did not come out of the house until family members came and talked her out.

This occurred nine days after giving birth to a six-month old, premature infant.

On the witness stand, Mr. Rico Gray lied about abusing his wife and causing her to be admitted into the hospital. He lied when he admitted that he was out of control and there was no telling what he would have done on that special day had she not discharged her weapon.

Mr. Rico Gray states that he had been lying to keep the mother of his daughter out of jail for twenty years. Marissa had been offered three years for the aggravated assault with a weapon, and this would have avoided the mandatory sentencing guidelines. It took the jury 12 minutes to come back with a verdict of guilty.

Her stand your ground hearing was lost and it was best for her to take the deal for three years.

Judge Elizabeth Senterfitt denied the "Stand Your Ground" petition which would have had the case thrown out. The judge stated Marissa could have exited another door but the law states that the person has no duty to retreat. The judge said that it appeared as if Marissa fired out of anger instead of fear. Her shot threatened the lives of her husband, and two innocent children.

Mr. Gray seems to be a low-key, perhaps, too even-tempered guy.

May 11, 2012

Marissa Alexander, the 31-year old AMS woman who fired what some considered as a warning shot at her abusive husband, was convicted of three counts of aggravated assault with a weapon and sentenced to twenty years in prison. Marissa is not an example of the mistreatment of blacks in the justice system of America. And due to mandatory sentencing guidelines, empathy and sympathy are not a part of the equation when people are on trial.

The husband later recanted his admission and stated that his wife has a violent nature; and it is her fault that she is doing time in prison. She was the one secretly communicating with her ex-husband. Her suffering, according to his latest statement, was due to her actions and not his physical abuse. Mother of three children, she apparently had, and has, a better relationship with her ex-husband, Lincoln, than with her estranged but current husband, Rico. An article dated June 13, 2013 stated that the fight for a retrial for Mrs. Alexander is ongoing.

The judge stated that his hands were tied and by Florida law, he had to rule using the "10-20-life" rule enacted under then-governor Jeb Bush, in 1999. Former governor Jeb Bush stated that the law was meant to catch the thug who robbed a store or committed a crime with the possession of a weapon. Those who think they are innocent take a chance and fall under the scrutiny of the rule and get the harsh penalties. Those who are guilty take the plea deal and receive far less time.

A November 21, 2013 article by Alexandra Thomas and an interview on HuffPost of Mr. Rico Gray brought some clarity to this complicated issue.

March 3, 3014

Alexander's retrial has created a rather precarious position for attaining her freedom. The same court that has ordered the retrial has also ruled that a conviction of multiple counts of the same crime, must result in consecutive sentences and not concurrent. In other words, in seeking to attain her freedom, Mrs. Alexander must now face the possibility of 60 years in prison instead of twenty. We need the federal court system to intervene because we are not quite free from a justice system that applies justice unevenly;

especially in the same state.

In the summer of 2002, Brian Banks was a football star with real hopes for going into the NFL. He was 6-foot-4 linebacker for his high school and he had received a letter of interest from several schools, including USC. He was 16 years-old when a childhood friend accused him of rape (she was 15). In a case where his word stood against the girl's word, he pleaded no contest to the rape charge, rather than risk 40-plus years in prison. He served five years in prison; and came out broke and just about unemployable. The charge was thrown out on Thursday, May 25, 2012. Since the supposed attack was stated as happening on the high school grounds, the female student accuser received a 1.5 million dollar settlement from the school system. That's quite a reward for lying and ruining a young man's dreams. But without the supposed victim's unofficial admission that Brian never raped her, he would not have his name exonerated. Brian is currently seeking money from the state for restitution and he still wants to play professional football.

No semen had been found on the young lady's underwear and there was a chance that he would have gotten off if the case had gone to trial. But the risk was just too great. This is another example of how the system fails to offer due diligence to AMS when we need the justice system to serve the people and convict those who are guilty and free those who are not.

The strategy of "oppose any minority issue" politics has long passed but someone needs to tell that to the politicians. The issue still raises its ugly head in the Trayvon Martin case. On August 3, 2013, the model of new racist thought masked in political rhetoric can be seen and heard in the actions and voices of the Tea Party. Florida Governor Rick Scott provides another angle to how to fan the flames of feigned righteous indignation instead of admitting you have done wrong. The governor demanded an apology from Civil Rights leader Rev. Jesse Jackson because brother Jackson compared the failings and misgivings of the Trayvon Martin case to the civil rights atrocities of Selma, Alabama.

The problem is that Tea Party politicians have gained access to the federal government on the backs of "no compromise" at all cost. Joe Walsh (R-Ill) is the leading example of being a product of the extremists who put him in office. He consistently makes negative references to people of color and still gets to voice his racist viewpoints from a political pulpit supported by media sound bites.

Thanks to HuffPost Black Voices online, I was able to hear one of his impassioned speeches in which he speaks of the Democrats wanting the "...Hispanic vote, they want Hispanics to be dependent on government , just like they got the African Americans dependent on government." That comment alone does not qualify Joe Walsh as the poster boy for the Tea Party movement. He makes several inflammatory remarks and these remarks are merely examples of him selling his soul to keep a job. His feigned passion is a contrived response to the hidden racist beliefs of those who support his wannabe political machine. He gets "wound up" for these people and is seemingly proud of it. But, no...this does not make him the poster child. Lawrence O'Donnell exposes Mr. Walsh for the hypocrite and sycophant that he really is. During an interview, Mr. O'Donnell asks Mr. Walsh if he would have voted against all 18 of the Ronald Reagan debt-ceiling increases. As he states that he doesn't know whether he would have done so, Mr. O'Donnell states that there might have been a debt-ceiling increase that Walsh would have voted for but he only emphatically opposes President Obama's debt-ceiling increases.

`The pattern is being revealed. No compromise when it comes to this President Obama who happens to be biracial and oddly enough the Tea Party people are continuously being fed racist remarks from Tea Party politicians. Now his resume for poster child of the Tea Party movement is gaining steam.

Mr. O'Donnell played a clip of Mr. Walsh's reasoning for not supporting the President's push to raise the debt-ceiling. He didn't want this debt put on the backs of "kids and grandkids unless we structurally reform the way this town spends money."

It's a YouTube video clip so listen for yourself at the morally principled, uncompromising politician who refuses to compromise solely because he is the last line of defense for keeping white Americans strong; i.e. white and males. After all what happens when white kids love the president; and little white girls like little black boys because a black President was in office when they were growing up...oh, my. I got sidetracked. Mr. O'Donnell states that mentioning your kids in a political statement makes your relationship with these kids fair game....so....he mentions that Joe Walsh, the moral heartbeat of America, has not paid over $117,000 dollars in child support for his kids while loaning his 2010 congressional campaign $35,000. Mr. Walsh has not explained how he got $35,000 to loan. While his campaign has paid him back about $14,000, he has not paid over several years of child support to the mother of his three children. Ouch! That's nasty. If he can get it for politics, why can't he get it for his children and clean up his personal life, which reflects on his political life. Oh, that's right! Tea partyers ignore their own foibles while castigating and judging others.

Well, one last tidbit as to why Mr. Joe Walsh, Republican out of Illinois, has the unofficial title of poster boy of the grand old Tea Party. Many men throughout America have problems with child support. My daughter is grown now but there were many things that I didn't and couldn't do as she grew older. But I didn't take my girlfriend to Mexico and Italy while failing to support my child. Yes, Mr. Walsh has managed to live a fairly nice life lately. He hasn't always had this kind of money and to be fair, perhaps his girlfriend has all the money. And that would be typical of the self-righteous Tea partyers as well. Congratulations, Mr. Joe Walsh on being the Poster Guy for the Tea Party.

Crooked Cops

Ex-Chicago cop **Jon Burge**, recently **given 4.5 years** for lying about knowing anything about a police torture ring that may have victimized more than 100 black men, will be allowed to keep his $3,039.03 per month pension, the police pension board ruled.

The African-American mistrust of local law enforcement has been due to systemic abuse and mistreatment of our people. Most

AMS people upwards of 40+ years of age, have experienced "bad cop behavior" at one time in their lives.

February 19, 2009

Brother Leroy Barnes was shot and killed by Pasadena, California police officers after a traffic stop. He had been riding along in the backseat of his friend's car. One news article states a young lady was driving the car. Police said they pulled the car over because Mr. Barnes looked like a gang member. Perhaps this was due to his riding in the backseat. The officers stated that Barnes had a gun and fired upon them; they returned fire and shot him eleven times (one officer shot seven times, the other officer shot 4 times). Apparently, Mr. Barnes, a reputed gang member, was not one of their better shooters because he missed at close range. As usual, most of the bullet wounds show that he was shot in the back. And as usual, the cops' version was a lie.

Police spokesmen revised the lie the next day. Police Chief Bernard Melekian attempted to straighten out the lie by saying that the victim fired once. The truth was the victim did not shoot one time; he was executed. One month later, the two cops involved in the shooting sued the city of Pasadena to prevent their names from being released, fearing retaliation from the Bloods gang members. On September 3, 2010, the courts lifted the ban of reporting the officers' names involved in the shooting. Officers Charles Glen Reep and Michael Alvarado were named in a wrongful-death lawsuit.

The entire scene was caught on dash-cam video but the department has refused to release the tape. I guess that tape doesn't clear this up in the police department's favor, eh? The department has stated that Barnes was a "convicted felon" and part of a gang. You will notice that police departments all across the country seem to think that a criminal record excuses the police from criminal charges after they execute a member of our community.

As frequently as this scene is being played out in America, one would think that police officers need to have their records revealed because surely some of them are straight-up racists from the get go. Barnes died without any CPR being administered at the scene. Of course, the police procedure is when you shoot, you need to kill because this precludes witnesses who would then have the opportunity to contest your version of the story. Sadly, this philosophy prevents the 'oops factor'...or slippers. *I shot once but it was a mistake. Instead we get dead brothers and hope and pray for a federal lawsuit.*

Pasadena Fires More Shots, Again

Kendrec McDade was a former high school football player who was shot seven times by police officers in Pasadena, California, on March 24, 2012. Seven days earlier, his mother, Anya Slaughter, had just given birth to his baby brother in Huntingdon Memorial Hospital. Now, on a Saturday night at about 11pm, Oscar Carillo called 911 to report that two armed men robbed him of his laptop and backpack while he while he was buying tacos at a taco truck. He later admitted lying about weapons in order to ensure quick police response. Kendrec was 19 years old. In our community, this is the age when young men are often seeking their way; trying to sift through the few options offered to them in recessive, racist, threatening economic times.

Officers Jeff Newell and Matthew Griffin, responded to the report that said it was an armed robbery. One officer followed on foot while the other officer drove the cruiser. The officer driving the cruiser shot Mr. McDade from the cruiser as he approached the officer. What happened to "Stay right there and remove your hand from your waistband!" The officer stated that Kendrec had his hand in his waistband; and this is becoming a common lie to reinforce excuses for shooting unarmed, young black men and children. Well, Kendrec died and the autopsy report released about two months later, reveals that he was shot seven times at close range and then handcuffed. The police chief has said that a security camera reveals that the two men were involved in the theft of Carillo's backpack; and that Kendrec served as the lookout. The 17-year old who admitted involvement with the crime has been sentenced by Pasadena Juvenile Court to six months in a camp community placement program. Kendrec's family denies that he was ever engaged in criminal activity that night. The AMS community is quite experienced with little pieces of misinformation (lies) that are released in order to substantiate the murder of members of our communities.

April 3, 2012

The parents of Kendrac McDade filed a wrongful-death and civil-rights lawsuit against the city. The suit alleges the officers never saw a gun, never shouted any warnings or commands, and handcuffed a dying man instead of offering assistance. Apparently, in lieu of reparations, the United States government has made plans to make restitution for centuries of oppression in our communities by means of lawsuits filed after killing off a number of AMS males.

In May of 2010, Chad Holley was apprehended for burglary after a chase by Houston police officers. He landed (after jumping in the air and being clipped by a police car) by a fence that surrounded some industrial building. The building also had video cameras posted. When Mr. Holley landed, four officers kicked and punched him. One officer kicked Holley in the head violently; another kicked him from the rear and all men know the danger of that. He also stepped on the back of his legs while he lay on the ground subdued.

One of the first officers who kicked him got in some kicks and took off running as if he wanted to get in some punk kicks before he answered another call. I found out later that this was officer Andrew Bloomberg. By the way, Chad Holley was 15 years old at the time of the assault.

It must be tough for officers to see the result of their master race oppression of African Americans. We were freed and shifted into second-class citizenry, crime, and drug-dealing and illegal gambling to make a living. The oppressor didn't want to work with or around blacks; and especially, for blacks. So, we couldn't get jobs to maintain the status quo. We found other avenues of rejecting the place that society demanded for us to settle. Now many urban criminals appear to be all black and the oppressors who created the iffy socio-economic situation In America, appear irritated. How does a real man, empowered by local government, punch another man who is defenseless? Answer. They are not men but some hybrid of local government officials, wild-west laws, insecurities, and oppressors.

How tough can it be when you know that prosecutor's will supply you with an all-white jury that will free you regardless of your transgressions. On Wednesday, May 16, 2012, despite the video evidence, now ex-Houston police officer Andrew Bloomberg (29) was acquitted of the beating of Chad — a video-captured beating.

Police Brutality in Chicago

Thursday, April 5, 2012, Howard Morgan was sentenced to forty years in prison. He is 61-years of age. Former Chicago police officer Howard Morgan (8 ½ years on the force) has learned that the thin blue line really never included him. After serving on the police force, Officer Morgan served for 13 years as a Railroad detective for the Burlington Northern Santa Fe Railroad. On the morning of February 21, 2005, on his way home, Howard Morgan was pulled over by some white police officers for driving the wrong way on a one-way street. The police officers say that he also had his lights off. He had worked at his job, had a late dinner at his wife's sister's home, and was now going to his home that was being remodeled.

The remodeling was the reason he and his wife were staying at his sister-in-law's home.

Okay, police officers; let's write him a citation and allow the man to go home. Was he drinking? Let's arrest him and keep him from hurting himself and/or others. Neither of these things happened; although he was eventually arrested. The white police officers say that after spotting the van with no lights; it ran three stop signs prior to being pulled over. Then, allegedly, Mr. Howard got out of the van and they came at him with guns drawn. They ordered him to place his hands on the van. While being patted down, they say that Mr. Morgan turned on them and began firing. They continued firing at Mr. Morgan, who was now on the ground, until he ran out of ammunition.

Mr. Morgan tells a completely different story. I'm glad his story is different because the cops' story sounds deficient; almost made up; as if someone had been watching a movie about chasing a secret agent. And no amount of cops and subjugation could conquer the hero. Mr. Morgan says that the police officers were behind him, so he slowed down to allow them to pass; but they wanted to stop him; so, they flashed their lights and pulled him over. After identifying himself as a police officer, four white rookie cops forced Howard Morgan from his vehicle, took his weapon and shot him 28 times. Twenty-one of those times were bullets that entered from his back and seven entered from the front in the chest and legs. The officers had forced him to the ground and shot him but claimed that he brandished his weapon and attempted to kill them. What? Was this guy crazy or what? I am sure that he was aware of proper police procedures once stopped; and that the Chicago Police Department receives about 2000 reports annually of police violence. Why would this guy do something so stupid? Answer: the cops are probably lying. Although he was never tested for gun residue on his hand...although his vehicle was crushed and destroyed prior to attaining any forensic evidence...although he was acquitted in 2007 of two counts of aggravated battery and the discharging of a firearm...although the state only produced 3 of the 28 bullets taken from Mr. Morgan's body...although the state never produced the bullet-proof vest worn by the officer who says he was shot...Mr. Howard Morgan, age 61, was convicted and sentenced to forty years in prison.

Mr. Howard underwent multiple surgeries to save his life. By God's grace and mercy, he survived; was handcuffed to a hospital bed for over six months and then transferred to jail. An anonymous donor put up the 2 million dollar bail. In the year of the incident (2005) his van was destroyed without notice or cause, prior to retrieving forensic evidence. The first jury trial (2007) acquitted Mr. Morgan of aggravated battery with a firearm and aggravated discharge of a firearm but deadlocked on attempted murder charges. Howard Morgan was convicted of attempted murder charges in a retrial in the spring of 2011. And you thought that carrying a gun and being on the side of law enforcement was a way of ensuring safety for your family and you. Mr. Morgan's wife and church and community are still fighting this battle. Visit freeHowardMorgan.com for more information. Visit the www.freehowardmorgan.com website for more information.

Shooting Black Girls in the Head

Ok. A great deal of law enforcement turmoil is happening in Chicago. On March 21, 2012, in the Lawndale neighborhood, a group had gathered and it was in the wee hours of the morning, around 1am. Off-duty officer Dante Servin, who apparently lives in the community, pulled up near the corner of 15th Place and Albany Avenue, and told the group to "shut up" with an urban expletive. A reply came from the crowd "FU", as in another urban expletive. A witness stated that officer Servin was raving in a manner to question the group about getting some quiet and respect from members of the community. And his answer was that he needed to shoot somebody to get respect. Well, he shot into the air and into the crowd for what is believed to be about six to ten times; striking

Rekia Boyd, 22, in the back of the head and shooting Antonio Cross, 39, in the hand. Rekia had just been visiting friends. She died the next day; she died because some guy wanted respect for being a police officer and a member of the community. Welcome, America to the front door of our downfall. Among the disenfranchised, the apathetic, the downtrodden...there was always respect for someone. Perhaps cops like Servin accelerated the demise of community respect with his past behavior. The officer states that he was in fear of his life as he exchanged words with Antonio Cross (who stated that he had a phone up to his ear and not a gun as the officer reported). This sounds so familiar. An aggressive, neighborhood police officer wants his community to have quiet in the wee hours of the morning; and not have people gathering around on the street corners. He desires the perception that where he lives is peaceful and law-abiding, mainly because he lives there. Ample amounts of testosterone flow during these types of confrontations. But there is also the possibility that the officer had been drinking. And no matter how much he feared for his life, it remains his responsibility where he discharges his weapon. He could just as easily have pulled away from the scene since there really was no police work for him to do. Antonio Cross is facing a misdemeanor count of aggravated assault so we can assume that police officials' initial claim of a gun at the scene were unsubstantiated and false.

Wednesday, June 11, 2013

The family of Rekia Boyd received $4.5 million dollars in a settlement from the Chicago City Council. She had no children so the money goes to her mother.

November 29, 2012

It happened in Cleveland, Ohio; the basketball home of Lebron James. Sixty police cars chased 43 year-old Timothy Russell and 30 year-old Malissa Williams after a police officer stopped the couple for driving erratically. The couple covered about 25 miles through highway I-90 and neighborhood streets and surely frustrated the numerous police officers involved in the high-speed chase. The couple was chased to the parking lot of Heritage Middle School in East Cleveland.

Allegedly, they were stopped because of suspicion of firing a gun from the car. Some say---and they didn't have a weapon---it was the car backfiring. While being stopped, the couple took off in the vehicle and almost struck three police officers who were on foot. This incident and striking a patrol car is considered assault or attempted murder; therefore, police officers feel justified to empty their guns on suspects. The unloading in this case amounted to 23 bullets in Mr. Russell and 24 bullets in Ms. Williams. Thirteen cops fired 137 shots to take their lives although they were unarmed. Stories abound concerning excessive force on AMS alleged criminal offenders.

The story ends with families grieving, funerals, and a lawsuit against the police department. Allegedly, Mr. Russell was legally drunk and Ms. Williams had been using drugs. Don't white folks get high and drive erratically? Sure they do. But we don't hear about them being shot twenty or more times.

Religion

The United States of America still sits as an experiment in the Western Hemisphere. Pale-skinned people left Europe, came to this continent and took it from the darker Native Americans, and nurtured the industries of this land using a still darker race of people from another continent as slave labor. The people who traveled here for religious freedom, eventually rode the path to freedom by taking the personal freedom of two races of people. Here is the rights argument in its earliest form for this country: the individual rights of a small segment of a sub-society were taken for the benefit of the larger base of society. That is an understatement.

This country has been a country of religious freedoms; it has never been a designated 'Christian' country. To declare it and to say it today is to say that the Christian faith has not been strong enough to prevent slavery; and it is not strong enough to stay the wicked course of governmental laws that break centuries of established moral guidance.

The individual rights of races of people, in order to achieve 'a more perfect union,' including personal security, religious freedom, and economic progress; were   hijacked by greedy people bent on making money from free land and labor. In their greed, they enslaved, brutalized, emasculated, raped, and slaughtered many of our African ancestors. Clearly, it was wrong. But what happened to that religion that they came to the country to pursue; freedom of religion?

Did it not carry basic tenements of most faiths: love others as you want to be loved? Christianity was the predominant religion but these precious holders of the right would invoke pretentious, bombastic language in declaring religious principles while turning a blind eye to slavery and its companions---torture, brutality, murder, and land thievery. The angst of guilt was so powerful that the Constitution declared Africans as less than human so that the business of free labor could continue; without having to bear the burden of guilt (saying it's okay to enslave people who were more like animals). It was perhaps, the birth of 'a convenient lie.' Later, the USA returned some land to the Native Americans and paid for other land; and offered some sweetheart deals through casinos. The USA has yet to attempt a compensatory action for African Americans other than unconstitutional affirmative action and minority set asides. Clearly, the verdict is still out on the great experiment that is the USA; some of which ironically have been ruled unconstitutional.

The clichéd statement is this country was built on Christian principles; and this is somewhat correct. It was built on the freedom to worship as you choose. Now Muslims are coming to this country of freedoms with some conflicting, radical, and committed beliefs; while we wrestle with God in favor of humanity's rights to do as it pleases.

Muslims, as a whole, are just faithful. They worship in the manner required by their faith; they wear what their religion requires, adhere to its strict diet; and openly demonstrate their faith in the workplace. If anything, the Christian liberalism generates conflict with so many other ideologies (especially religious ones) because so many 'believers' make loose commitments to God. These loose religious commitments make it more difficult for truly faithful people to assimilate. In other words, they see our versions of religion, they see the liberalism in sex, alcohol consumption, and conduct and question our commitment to God. As any committed person who perceives wrong all-around, he or she seeks to protect their family against unrighteousness.

So, the natural transfer of religious power seems imminent because political correctness suppresses the less demanding, less vindictive and less demonstrative, Christian faith. The religion that demands the most from society has to receive some concessions or the great guilt complex that is this country's, will suffer. By the way, that guilt complex is evident for everything and everybody except for Christians and reparations for descendants of slaves. How odd.

Generations of civilizations have chosen to have a religion as the predominant teacher and sustainer of morals and principles; and it has been fairly effective. Some people look to avoid specific sins on their holy days; and some take courses and studies to maintain a spiritual perspective despite the concerns of the world. Even dictatorships maintain a central moralistic identity based in the very will of the dictator's will. When a country takes the high road in the area of moral responsibility, a determined will of moral fiber will emerge and become dominant; usually in rebellious confusion from not having one present.

Abortionists say what they want and society makes concessions to the tune of 600,000 potential births a year. We are paying for those actions. Margaret Sanger, the founder of Planned Parenthood, was an intellectual racist who advocated for the extermination of minorities and ethnic groups who did not provide a benefit to society but brought society down. She actually referenced Negroes and the need for racial purity. She believed in limiting (if not exterminating) inferior races so as not to deter the progress of her race. She used community Baptist preachers to convince AMS that abortion was "planned parenthood" and not a quest for extermination.

It is no coincidence that Planned Parenthood has the great majority of its locations in urban/minority communities; and stands boldly on the philosophies of its founder. Now, the group has tremendous resources other than providing for abortions but their most brazen mission is highly unacceptable.

In poetic injustices found in life, Planned Parenthood resembles the N-word. It is a societal metaphor for needlessly casting enduring psychological and physical pain upon the innocent. It's a label that wants to justify itself instead of being eradicated. We know of its disrespect and its purpose was clearly stated; there was nothing good about it. There have always been alternatives.

The message is clear: minorities need help planning child birth because no one wants a whole bunch of them running around. T

he message prevailed until we accepted it and incorporated it as helping to prevent, and eliminate, unwanted pregnancies. Now our communities are having more abortions than childbirths while our Hispanic brothers and sisters are doing the opposite for political, religious, and socially-strategic gain.

In Texas (June-July 2013), the issue was raging about a restrictive anti-abortion law which would effectively ban abortions after 20 weeks (five months); and close most clinics in the state. For such a controversial measure, there is nothing wrong with making someone drive a little farther to take a life; and it really makes sense that after a certain time, no one should be authorized to kill almost fully-formed babies.

Flesh-driven, practical society creates a miraculous method for females who want a baby to have a baby but that method creates millions of fertilized embryos that must be frozen or destroyed. Once in vitro is completed, the unneeded tubes of embryos will become full-term babies; so, they must be destroyed or frozen until later usage is found. What in the world is that? It has been the promise of life that makes existence so mysterious and wonderful; so, let's just trash that promise and process and admit confusion as to its beginnings. A woman who can't have a baby, through wondrous technological and biological advancements, can have a fertilized egg taken from a test tube and inserted inside her. But the process creates another dilemma because she only wants one or two babies and there is no guarantee as to how many eggs will become fertilized. The value of life weakens as the spirit of selfish, individual rights weakens a formerly uncompromising but righteous stance. We are paying; each soul bears the weight of policies that devalue life, and allow us to think of life as readily disposable as long as it is not ours. Each soul pays a price.

As in most civilizations, religious fanaticism provides a cure for many of the ills of society; while sometimes overriding individual rights. Those looking from the outside tend to perceive the religious direction as fanatical since a woman is entitled to do what she will with her body.

In America, we choose individual rights over the systemic woes once kept at bay by religion. A religious person may consider the issue of abortion if his or her teenage daughter gets pregnant without a husband. Muslims will accept individual freedoms until it conflicts and contests the values of Islam. Then, no reflection is needed because Islam trumps individual rights. In other words, faith in God involves a commitment that has nothing to do with how you are perceived. In Christianity, we are encouraged to not be conformed to the world but be transformed by the renewing of our minds.

Christians are considered radical for something that is easy for us to see. We are basically killing babies on a large scale because many women, men, girls, and boys, got caught up in the moment and fail to take preventive measures to prevent conception. Hispanics are flooding this country and having babies in great numbers. They bring their children into American schools with double-strollers and an older sibling holding the hands of two toddlers.

AMS is getting played/taken advantage of/ messed over. We lead in the number of abortions but our Hispanic brothers and sisters know that babies born in this country are United States citizens, entitled to all of the benefits of a citizen. Forget the national debate about abortions and take a more personal perspective: we (AMS) need more babies born in this country.

Our quest to assimilate in this country has deceived us into thinking that we are exactly like mainstream American citizens. No, we don't need to reproduce irresponsibly in some mad quest to become the majority in America. But we do need to rebuild the moral foundation in our communities to appreciate life. There is a seed connection in taking life and in finding it easy to murder each other. If abortion clinics are only in minority communities, remove them or put them in Caucasian communities and see how long these clinics will exist.

Yes, we know and understand the special situations concerning incest, rape, delivery risks, and deformities (upon which a Christian would still need to pray).

The Affordable Care Act or what is known as ObamaCare, has stipulations that employees pay for health care and this has included birth control with specific plans. The Supreme Court of the United States ruled on June 30, 2014 that some companies with religious objections can refuse to be bound by the birth control requirement. This decision involved the company, Hobby Lobby, that didn't want to pay for specific birth control methods which were more closely related to abortion.

For mainstream America, including many liberals, this is an affront against the rights of women and it seems to support companies picking and choosing specific parts of the ACA that they don't want to support financially. If we were in a Muslim country, specific rulings such as the aforementioned would make sense. Every now and then, a religious issue should be prioritized ahead of individual rights. And at face-value, the issue appears fair since the company is agreeing to pay for other contraceptive methods.

These are examples of devaluing life in America. Systematically we are slicing away the institutions that support family, morals, and perpetuation of the species. Is Christianity the perfect institution to mentor American morality? Perhaps not; but it is better than having a religion filled with zealots, desiring to fight immorality and unrighteousness with bombs; while killing teenage daughters who rebel in attitudes and dress. Yes, religion is rigid on many issues. Yes, organized religion may seem like a con to many. But religion redeems murderers in the prisons and out of prisons; it saves marriages, and teaches children to fear God because he is always watching them. Yes, some Christians murder, and divorce is often just as high among Christians but the benefit of the systematic instruction for civility, morality, and obedience far outweighs the alternatives that America seems to gravitate towards.

When we took prayer out of schools it was throwing out the baby with the bath water. Although most of the founders of this country were so religious that they spoke of some say we should not teach religion in schools but we need moral values in place; and having God over this system provides assurance and amazement that it is constantly being watched. Ancient Chinese civilizations promoted religions just to keep tribal wars from decimating the country.

Christianity teaches grace and mercy and forgiveness but there are Christians among us who bear the burden of being tougher and more stringent when it comes to the word of God. We of the faith understand the individual calling and we cast no judgment but those who don't practice the faith consider it anti-Christian to straight-up reject some compromises.

So, President Barack Obama "evolved" on the issue of same-sex marriage; the word of God has not changed. Christians may understand why people accept gay marriage: friends, coworkers, relatives, and associates are members of the LBGT community and it is quite natural to desire to show support for passionate issues, with those we know and interact. But the word of God does not change; and it has delivered people beyond many wicked, false ideologies that they once believed.

Kirk Cameron used the words 'unnatural' and 'destructive' to describe homosexuality and you would have thought that he committed an egregious sin. He restated a well-traveled and biblically-taught spiritual philosophy regarding homosexuality. Modern society has the right to say that the teaching is wrong; and since many religions, people, and countries still view homosexuality as wrong, it is not as if the Bible's teachings are outdated.

Modern social engineering has chosen to favor approving of homosexual behavior while some of the spiritually-enlightened followers of biblical scriptures have chosen to maintain the belief expressed in the Bible. There is no conflict with the political concept of individual sexual rights and God's law. We believe the law is stated and it is your choice to follow it or not. If the new political-social movement were not trying to eradicate Christian thought, it is a strong possibility that people would evolve to understand Christians support of biblical concepts.

I think American society is missing some vital commonsense issues. No, we are not afraid of homosexuality being taught in schools right now. But what happens when children make increasingly distasteful, and hurtful comments about parents who have 'come out'? The more people who come out, the more such conflicts will arise among children. The next move will be to educate the children about sexual choices (as a result of seeking to stop bullying) and learning to love each other and how to simply interact with others despite differences.

Simple it seems. But at this time, sexual choice would be introduced to children who are not yet motivated by biological drive. The introduction becomes a tool for making social decisions. Is this boy a friend or a boyfriend to be? When the child becomes older and aware of how his sexual choices impact companionship, he may be encouraged to reason and question the type of relationship he has developed. In 2014, the majority of children don't have to face such reasoning because their interactions are defined clearly as friendship and this friendship may involve discussing the opposite sex.

Perhaps, a more indirect lesson will be delivered by commercials and songs, and movies depicting sexual mores of a society. Society has a right to choose how it wants its children to be indoctrinated; yet, lawsuits will abound regarding who has a right to show and promote various relationship-types on television; and in schools.

When society talks religion, people like the idea of cherry-picking concepts and rejecting those philosophies with which large groups of individuals don't agree. In religious thought, that is an aberration; we accept the religion, all of its doctrine, and teachings. Major issues are resolved in prayer; and conflict is spiritually resolved in the counsel of like-minds bound together by the Spirit of God. The Christian faith has a plethora of concepts and doctrine that has been evaluated, reviewed, and validated.

Even Jesus turned over a few tables out of outrage over what some Jewish believers had contrived within the parameters of faith for the purpose of making money. Even Jesus called out a traitor to the cause of faith. His love was based on the hope for every person to attain and prioritize personal salvation ahead of personal feelings and systemic ideologies. It is a common goal of our fleshy sins to reason right where none exists; and ignore right when the desire to do wrong deeply impacts our soul.

November 7, 2012

In the state of Maryland, the same-sex marriage law passed (it was pushed as a marriage equality law which was smart) and the majority has spoken. Expansion of gambling operations was also passed.

Society wants to marginalize Christianity in favor of accepting many religions and lifestyles. Yet, society needs to reflect upon the consequences of removing faith-based policies. Without a national religion, we are subject to the influences of the more persistent or forceful religion.

Someday, not too far in the future, this country will be forced to adopt Islamic holidays and stringent policies, at least in specific communities. We will have Little Arabia, Little Iran, or Little Iraq communities. The concept of "The Great Melting Pot" would have been fully realized.

Perhaps that day would not be as bad if we could maintain a fairly consistent moral foundation; but that will change as well. These communities will have their own cultural and highly ethical policies that will thrive in such tight-knit, religious communities. And clearly, there will be cast, good versus evil. The decadent society will stand against the ethical and intensely devout; albeit radical and replete with extremist factions. Surely, righteous indignation of moral laxity will steadily increase in this country; and surely, as in Egypt, Yemen, and Syria, there will be cries for social and perhaps, political, revolution.

In other words, when Muslim men bring their children to this great country and witness the moral lack that is prevalent here, they maintain as much of their moralistic ways as possible to maintain a respectful, obedient, and decent live-style for their family. Society, as it stands, confirms the need for them to form rigid, strict, communities instead of fully assimilating. If I brought my children to this great country from a religious Middle Eastern country, you better believe that it would make sense for me to have them maintain specific aspects of my faith; even those that tend to promote an ultraconservative position.

Unfortunately, when daughters dishonor fathers with inappropriate attire, dressing in skimpy clothes, or by having sex prior to marriage, fathers may reflect upon old school methodologies for rendering correction: sharia law in which such dishonor deserves death. The confusion reigns for these fathers because their adopted country has such wonderful freedoms that consistently tempt and misguide their children.

Must a father sit back and do nothing to discipline a wayward child when his new country promotes the tight pants and skimpy dresses, and promiscuity? Even a prominent mega-church pastor had an issue with a disobedient daughter and in comparison to sharia law, he allegedly handled it in evenhandedly.

Television, abortion, clothing, saying the pledge, homosexuality, profanity-laced music, marijuana laws, education, holidays, dating, marriage, and every aspect of society opens the door for various cultural interpretations that conflict with good old American ways. We fail to look into the future and benefits of Christian faith: people may offer concessions to a religion but where none is present, they must strongly advocate their own.

Christianity should be used to reduce fanaticism. Sure there is the Westside Baptist church that is not Baptist affiliated but supports fanatical persecution of gays and soldiers; but that is the exception. This country needs to support Christianity simply to reduce chaos; and yes, it is self-serving for Christians but it reduces other problems. It offers our Middle East immigrants a viable substitution for assimilation of their children into a wickedly permissive society.

Oddly, we support Israel because of Judeo-Christian beliefs. Yet, we don't proclaim ourselves to be a Christian nation (we should at least have a religious identity) and we fail to understand that in not projecting a religious identity, some group is eager to give us one; and it may not be one that is tolerant of other faiths.

Yassir Zyaed supposedly killed his two daughters as an honor killing. Apparently, these good law-abiding Muslims kill their children if they become too westernized; yet, to fully and dutifully assimilate, it must be done one generation at a time. Those who gather together to maintain the old ways (honor killings) will be persistent because American society must not even mention the phrase "honor killing" least we offend, while mistakenly enlightening people as to the misguided mindset that encourages such a philosophy. It must be called for what its participants' purposed it so that the world can know the potential devastation of one erroneous unchecked thought.

The Christian-Political-Racial Dilemma
November 17

Pat Robertson always allows his Republican conservative fangs to show. Most people I know think like I think. We don't support capital punishment but if someone we love gets abused or killed we understand the potential influence of emotional misgivings. We don't believe in abortion and gay rights but we want the best for Brother KiKi and Cousin Shawn; and the church pianist. On many of these issues, Pat Robertson may find some agreement in the AMS community. But he, like a few other big-time televangelists, loves to spout off about his politics. And to bring AMS into the sordid picture, they take our social causes and politicize them so they can accuse us of being just as, if not more, political.

The politics of religious conservatism is no simple matter. Conservative politics and values oddly conflict with social justice and caring about the underprivileged. Yes, conservatives value life so no abortions, please. Yes, conservatives value life, so no capital punishment please. Oh, no. if you commit a crime that requires death, you should be put to death quickly. Forget about the disparities and false testimonies that have led to black convictions for murder.

Pat Robertson stated that President Obama has a "Muslim inclination" and then rattled off about how he has an African and Indonesian background as some sort of vague ideological proof of this inclination. These religious Christian men always amaze me. We (Christians) can't alienate our brothers for such trifling reasoning. President Obama also attended a Roman Catholic school and he has repeatedly...repeatedly stated that he is a Christian. What makes politics so important that we run the risk of alienating those whose souls obviously need nurturing?

Yet, evangelicals such as Franklin Graham can show compassion on the white man candidate, Mitt Romney, who is really not a Christian but a Mormon. Franklin Graham knows this but took down the declaration of Mormonism as a cult from his website, in order to endorse Mr. Romney in his bid for the presidency of the United States. Why such forgiveness for one and not the other? Could it be that the prospect of this liberal man of color having another term in the White House was so repudiating that the man of God changed his beliefs about basic requirements to be called Christian?

Mormonism has been rife with racism and beliefs that contradict the teachings of the Bible. The Bible had been around for thousands of years and in 1830, here comes a new translation by Joseph Smith called the book of Mormon. No other book shares authority for Christian teachings; especially one that has to face updating due to its racist propaganda. That's why Christians believe solely in the Bible.

Now, I understand that the President does not appear to be as enthusiastic a Christian as former President George Bush but that is no reason to consistently throw him under the bus and to create a bus when there is none. At least he professes Christianity. These guys can't handle Democratic Christians who have an agenda of making some concessions to the poor and oppressed of society. When the issue is politics, they speak of religion; and when the primary issue is religion, they speak of politics. If they maintained some consistency, we would find that Jesus Christ puts us all on the same battlefield; but we have to be willing to limit the distractions.

It is a preparatory exercise in the futility of the Republican frontrunner, Mitt Romney. Evangelicals and Holy Spirit-filled Christians share something that is uncommon in these times: we believe in God; we believe that the Bible is the undisputed, word of God; and we believe that it is our mission to offer salvation to the world, induced through the Holy Spirit in the name of Jesus Christ. We know that many have not been touched by the Spirit of God and they have a perfunctory belief. But it is still a good thing to have religion and it is still a good thing to attend church.

We who have been communing with God, know that evil comes across many methodologies to seek the conquest of our souls. It is no coincidence that the Presidential Election of 2012 examined the role of a president who has been rendered ineffective by the opposing party in favor of a contender who is a Mormon. That's right. The evangelicals prioritize godliness and godly missions ahead of everything; so, a Mormon running against a Christian (no matter the degree of devoutness) is a spiritual no-brainer. Unless other factors such as racism creep into the decision-making process.

Some evangelicals will use the argument that President Obama is not a practicing Christian due to political issues that he supports: gay relationships and abortion. Some evangelicals and devout Christians cannot wrap themselves around such issues and have no consternation about what is right and what is wrong. But we know that lukewarm Christians and those less devout may exercise various aspects of reasoning to compromise their decisions regarding these seemingly tough issues. I would like to think that it matters how much the President lacks in devotion because as long is in the fold, he can easily achieve enlightenment on these issues. But I would hate to be the President who improved America's ability to have abortions, to smoke dope, and to marry people of the same-sex. It smells of hedonism and with the lack of Congressional assistance, the aforementioned accomplishments might declare his legacy.

Lastly, we all put specific beliefs aside in favor of adjusting our spiritual lives to fit and give more credence to our secular world. It became a spiritual issue for AMS to have the same rights as everyone else. Homosexuals are trying to add some spiritual components to their battle for rights. Conservative political activists want to cloud social and racial disparities with governmental policy and a unified conservative Christian front. If the issue conflicts with the Spirit of God's word, it cannot be supported in righteousness.

That statement is not as vague and ambiguous as it appears. Social justice was a strong tenant of Jesus Christ. He spoke to people whom his religion banned contact; he professed love for all; and he professed marriage as between male and female (Matthew 19:4); while calling out specific sins as sins.

Friday, April 14, 2012

So, here comes Richard Land of the Southern Baptist Convention. Mr. Land quoted from Jeffrey Kuhner's March 29 Washington Times Op-Ed and this information was attained via an article by Greg Horton, Religious News Service (April 17, 2012). Apparently, the comparison was made between Ku Klux Klan leaders and civil rights leaders, including the President of the United States. Mr. Land has boasted of tripling the number of AMS members from around 350,000 in 1995 to close to one million members today. Land made a comment stating that President Barack Obama "poured gasoline on the racialist fires" when he commented on Trayvon Martin's slaying. That is a bit of a stretch to say that any president cannot make comments about any situation regarding the social and political conscience of America. Mr. Land

149

also accused President Obama, the Rev. Jesse Jackson and the Rev. Al Sharpton of using the case "to try to gin up the black vote for an African American president who is in deep, deep, deep trouble for re-election." Mr. Land predicted violence would be the result of supporting such righteous causes in the African American community. Sounds like, "ya"ll just shut up and be good boys and girls while the master sorts this thing out for everybody."

First point, oh, Great White Wannabe Religious Leader for African Americans, this is about unjust social and criminal profiling; it is about unfairness, political and social; it is about not establishing social elements to correct errors of the past; and it is about religion...yes, religion, that says love your neighbor; be considerate in dealing with others. It always amazes me how religious conservatives can't seem to see beyond race when they simply need to apply religious concepts to dealing with others. Mr. Land needs to accept the cultural boundaries encompassing him based on his own lack of AMS experiences. By increasing the membership of AMS in his church, he is profoundly proclaiming the "I have black friends" excuse when being called a racist...knowing that they are not really friends. If he had a clue, he would not have made such comments about historical matters on which he has a very limited perspective.

Secondly, the only reason President Obama is perceived to be in trouble for re-election is due to the right-wing politicians who have tried to turn everything he has attempted to accomplish into some misguided, political contest. Has he handled the situation in the best way? No one knows because there has never been an AMS President of the United States who has had to deal with what ultimately results in the tragic demise of the "good ol' boy network."

There is no compromise with this group of politicians because any success may mean that we need more men like the President in office. Agreeing with the President may sound the death kneel on white Conservatives throughout the country. Supporting the President may unleash an unbridled sense of overcompensation of fairness; electing dark and brown officials solely based on the color of their skin. So the white men of the religious right are fighting for their ultra-conservative lives.

Is It All About Sex?

On September 25, 2010, a fourth young man came forth to say that Bishop Eddie Long coerced him into a sexual relationship. This dominated the news headlines for a week. Initially, two young men came forth to say that he used his influence as pastor and mentor to engage them in a relationship. The last young man stated that he was 15 when he engaged in a sexual relationship with the bishop.

Sunday, September 26, 2010

Bishop Long spoke before his congregation and stated that he has been accused and attacked; and misrepresented in the media. He didn't deny anything and he stated that his lawyers told him to not try this case in the media. The human part of me felt that he had not given enough to his congregation nor to me. As a man, if I had a bully pulpit to address accusations that will mess with the minds of thousands if not millions of Christians, I would have to say something like "I'm a man and have always been...I would not risk this ministry with such a debasing situation; I sleep with women only...right now it's just my wife and that's forever." Instead, the bishop referred to not being a perfect man three times. A little too much self-deprecating; as if to say there is something you will find out but it is not this thing. His wife sought to divorce him, but changed her mind.

The speculation can become all-consuming. I prefer not to

speculate but to state that someone will pay for this tremendous explosion against faith.

AMS culture has taken on the religion of the former oppressor and magnified it and glorified it to help in fulfilling its purpose as a beacon of light for the oppressed, stricken, and lost. One man cannot declare, represent, or stain our faith or religion.

In the Bible, the Ethiopian eunuch traveled to Jerusalem and read the words of the Old Testament (Isaiah) and the apostle Philip converted him to Christianity; and it is believed that he had status in his society so he took the Gospel back to Ethiopia. There is a second century statue depiction of the Virgin Mary and the baby Jesus that hails from Ethiopia. Needless to say, it is not the oppressors' religion and we are not wayward ancestors of former slaves blindly obeying any shyster that comes to town.

We also don't forgive blindly; although by faith it is what should be done. Our assessment of our faith is that it is bigger than any one man; including the pastor of a mega-church who grew the church over the last 20 years from 150 members to 25,000+. Allow me to rephrase that: a man who God used to grow the church into a membership of 25,000+. The outcome is greater than his sin but it does not mean that he should be allowed to escape punishment if he is guilty.

The pictures that were sent to one of the young men has no obvious sexual impropriety. It appears a little odd that the bishop would send pictures of himself to the young man. They showed the bishop standing up with form-fitting body wear in one picture and a form-fitting shirt in another. The email that one young man posted is from him to the bishop and it basically says that the bishop hurt him. There is nothing to offer a hint of a sexual relationship.

Bishop Long preaches and teaches that homosexuality is a sin. The truth is that he is married and he has been preaching the word of God. So, even with his sexuality in question, he preaches the Bible and that does not evolve the church's position on homosexuality. The bishop preaches the wonderful aspects of marriage yet he has been divorced.

One could argue that religion in the AMS community is one of the most sacred, misunderstood institutions in the world. It is a complex blend of faith, humor, ritual, financial empowerment, entertainment, sacredness, and community that blends more distinct systems than any other institution in the world. God blesses some earthly vessels with great communicative skills that intertwine the complexities of society in heartfelt messages of the Gospel.

We laugh at our own sense of holiness; but we seek to become even more holy. We seek a holiness that accepts our own sins without judgment, while we know that we are supposed to desire to commit less sin. We laugh at our foibles that come to light ever so often because we know that everyone has a few; but we pray that it will not cause a great stir. We laugh as the preacher admits his own weaknesses without confession of the details but we really want to know exactly what it is. And we know that if we find out what it is, we will have trouble not judging him because we expect him to be so much better than the rest of us.

The dilemma presented by the Bishop's scandal is beyond a simplistic case of veracity and sexual innuendo. In revealing such sexual accusations, the young men were at best setting the bishop up for a settlement if he is guilty; and perhaps, if he is not guilty. The settlement was reached on May 27, 2011. The federal and state authorities refused to prosecute because the young men were of the age of consent in Atlanta. Their lawsuit sounds like the American dating scene: a man who had power, influence, and wealth, made himself approachable to teenage boys and eventually seduced them. Or, a man of power, influence, and wealth made himself approachable to some young teenage boys and eventually, they took advantage of him. With the threat of incarceration removed from the table, the pastor's maturity, decision-making, and sexual desires had to be discussed among board members, who would represent the direction of the church body. A vote may have been cast and that's where a church family reflects a true family. Their decision, their business.

The church's decision would involve spiritual principles and

Christian dogma concerning adultery and fornication; and the consideration for risk of other male teenagers under the pastor's ministerial leadership. The church membership was willing to forgive and continue by faith. Some churches and church leaders make it through such chaos and some don't.

Every good preacher should get to the point of preaching against something he or she still has a problem with in heeding God's command. No one is perfect and only God knows the heart, and true repentance. The congregation or board made a decision to keep the bishop on his post.

Could all of this be a doorway for placement of our homosexual brothers and sisters within the church? After all, they have been playing instruments and singing and leading choirs for decades and spiritual presence is still being maintained. Do we need this relationship to change? Does this incident mark a betrayal of the church's version of "Don't Ask, Don't Tell"?

Episcopalians have prepared the way for accepting homosexual religious leaders but no other major religious group that I know of has changed their stance about homosexuality.

Is the bishop a practicing homosexual leading a major church or is he a repentant homosexual who admits that he cannot lead contrary to the word of God; or is he a homosexual who will do the best that he can to abstain?

At question is the role of the church in African-American communities in modern times where states are passing laws for same-sex marriage. Homosexuals are growing in power and representation in the country, and the church usually makes it clear that we welcome all sinners. Hence, the white elephant in the room: we consider homosexuality as a sin that needs to be suppressed and corrected by the Holy Spirit, individually. Biblically speaking, openly gay in church is like saying I am a liar, hater, law-breaker, flirt, drug addict and/or gambler and I plan to stay that way; as a matter of fact, I'm sinning right now in front of you and I'm planning to really get things popping as soon as church is over. Oddly, we do have people who commit various sins who live by this philosophy.

In following the Bible, I dislike being considered homophobic. As Christians, we love the sinner and hate the sin. By faith, we consider homosexuality as a sin while many homosexuals proclaim they are born in this condition. OK. The Bible says: "Behold, I was shapen in iniquity; and in sin did my mother conceive me" (Psalms 51:5). We have the mindset and direction to grow into adulthood and make decisions for which we are responsible.

Now, all sinners have been in many situations in which we want to make excuses for sinning. This is our flesh. Until that is resolved within us, usually, we hide our sins; unless our sins become so powerful that we become convinced of their authority in our lives and refuse to hide them.

Some people drink and get high before church. Liars will lie during a sermon; and gamblers will try to sponsor church trips to Atlantic City to raise money for the building fund. So, the homosexual push for acceptance is not so shocking.

Sinners can be used to give a message, to bless the righteous, to provide guidance in specific areas. It is not right to throw one's sins before him or her as if to seek correction by the power of my proclamation. But, if the sin is constantly thrown in my face, it is my spiritual responsibility to address it; and watch God do the rest.

My wife and I had a spiritual revelation in our home at the kitchen table. We placed an altar near the kitchen next to the living room. When we moved, we placed the altar in a similar position in our larger home. We also mention quite often, the two women who played a role in reintroducing us to spiritual commitments. In spiritual revelation, the messenger, the place, the scripture, and the time become endearing aspects of the supernatural experience.

Yes, we have a tremendous amount of respect for the man of God but it is a natural, supernatural consequence of having faith. We are not fools; we are forgivers who follow God's word. When God connects with us through a vessel (human or otherwise) we have a tremendous amount of respect for the vessel.

Bishop Long's congregation, on February 3, 2012, perhaps in

rebellion and defiance to the scrutiny their Christian family fellowship had received, allowed a Jewish Christian rabbi, Ralph Messer, to proclaim the leadership of the bishop and declare him as a king. It was quite a ceremony. Although there is no Jewish coronation ceremony in which someone is wrapped in the Torah and made a king, the fellowship most assuredly had a good reason for this interpretive ceremony.

Yes, our respect and love for God may easily transfer to the vessel but it is not a bad thing as long as we frequently reflect upon the godly reason the vessel became significant in our lives. The human vessel will always be flawed but the ministry that God has used the vessel to perpetuate has become supernaturally imbued. Every minister, in every pulpit is unworthy of the calling that has placed him or her behind that sacred desk but by the grace of God. This grace has been attained by faith and in accepting Jesus Christ as Savior these same ministers become qualified for their godly assignment, despite their many, varied shortcomings.

Rev. Al Sharpton Supports Same Sex Marriage in Maryland

February 10, 2012, Rev. Al came to the aid of the same-sex marriage cause recently generated as a political smokescreen by Governor Martin O'Malley and the Democratic Party. Many of us in the state of Maryland cannot figure why a lame-duck governor would take on the cause of higher taxes and same-sex controversies; despite the need to address lack of jobs and economic stagnation. I guess those don't paint a pretty picture of his job performance although most of the country has the same problems.

Oddly, his stances appear to evolve with the Democratic/Presidential platform. Of course, Eureka! It came to me like God had dropped it directly into my spirit. He is still politicking because he wants to continue in politics as high up as he can go.

Gov. Martin O'Malley is a decent looking, highly personable, white male...perhaps the presidency one day, he wants. But what about Rev. Al? Al Sharpton was almost like a modern-day hero (for me), until his stance and aggressiveness on same-sex marriage evolved; prompting him to travel to Maryland to fight a battle that the Bible clearly addresses. What does he have to gain speaking against the scriptures in a state that is not his state? Did he ever study the Bible after preaching his first sermon at age 4?

It is definitively a theological, moral, socialization issue that many seek to turn into a civil issue. Marriage is a civil right that was strategically placed under the auspices of the church because of the overriding issues attached to it. Property and finances, child-rearing, health issues (especially when one needs long-term care or dies) societal status, stability (careers), legal contracts, and uniquely monogamous love will need to be addressed in the average marriage and only one institution had the framework to cover such a multitude of issues.

I got married in the courthouse and had my vows renewed in church five years later. The Rev. Donte "Can I Preach It Like I Feel It?" Hickman, who my wife and I used to watch every Sunday morning on television, made the stance that civil marriage which is proposed is not the same as traditional marriage...he can support civil marriage...but he will not conduct such marriages in his church. That makes a lot of sense for you, Rev. Donte; for you, Rev. Donte, for you. He might as well have not said anything and stated his neutrality.

And the confusion for followers of Jesus Christ in America grows. I understand the confusion. The Bible clearly states that some things are not allowed and yet people don't have a problem with allowing these things. Why come so strongly against homosexuality when some preachers support it and even believers selectively disobey many directives of the Bible?

Rev. Al now has a girlfriend, and with common sense rationale he declares:" Don't I have a right to date when my marriage has been over for over a decade?" He was married for over 24 years and in 2004 they became legally separated; but he is still married as they have not gotten divorced. The concept is not simply the fact that he is legally married. It is as a Christian, your behavior impacts others and you run the risk of leading others astray in the area of marriage and adultery. Why can't I have a girlfriend since my wife and I have slept in different beds for one month? Why can't I have a boyfriend since my husband spends several nights a week traveling and when he is home he pays me no attention?

The religious standard helps to avoid confusion for many, including the un-churched, and Reverend Al should know this. The church standard is always about what is best for faith in Jesus Christ for those in the world, in its commitments and in its desires. Yes, the church has made some mistakes but overall, it has a foundation for making improvements, compromises, and concrete assessments. The church has had sexual deviant priests but it does not support sexual deviancy. All those who say, Lord, Lord, shall not enter into the kingdom of heaven. When slaves were in the fields being oppressed by the slave master, they would sing: ev'rybody talkin' 'bout heaven, at goin' to heaven, heaven.

How difficult it would be for me to contradict God's word and advocate a secular stance on such a major issue. Emotionally, children will connect with their inexplicable hormonal urges (you couldn't explain it to them if you tried) and make emotional, sexual decisions. A little boy got some nationwide media coverage when he read a letter supporting same-sex marriage. What the heck does a fifth-grader really know about marriage or sex, other than some Internet pictures? What happens when little boys start bringing their little boyfriends home, holding hands. *No, Mom, this is not my friend, this is my boyfriend.* And no, they don't have the extra chromosome, and they are not gay. They are simply exercising a choice based on what is offered to them as children of a free-loving society. Now, in their childhood memories, when they reflect, the heterosexual who has been with someone of the same sex because he or she didn't understand will be angry. Our adolescents who become adults will reflect the most confusing aspects of learned and unlearned sexual activity.

But what about the church? What role is it to play in this massive swirl of confusion? It must stand up to the forces that seek to immobilize us. We must stand just because someone is pushing against what we believe; and we have a right to believe as we do.

We can show a tremendous outpouring of love and say come on and feel welcomed despite a lack of reformation and repentance. Or we can introduce them to the word and the Spirit and proclaim that all sinners do wrong and that's why you are surrounded by such a cloud of witnesses. The church will surround them with people who have proclaimed their unrighteousness along with their desire to improve.

After all, the homosexual issue came out as a statement for being true to self and not being ashamed. Then it grew into having established relationships that wanted to be treated as marriages. Then it grew with the excuse that the treatment as marriages would provide marital benefits and the same benefits as other marriages. And everyone backpedaled because these issues made sense and we all knew some members of the LBGT whom we had befriended, worked with, or to whom we were related, and we did not really want to offend. Now, it is such a powerful group that political commentators cannot even make jokes about them without it coming across as a homophobic slur. Sorry, Roland Martin.

They have an unfair advantage in the political arena because no one is allowed to say anything against them. Political commentators representing Tea Party views have lambasted AMS and put that old racist stigma on us about food stamps and handouts; and have even gone as far as attacking the wife of the President and her body parts. Yet, one brother makes an indirect comment about slapping some people who look at men's underwear and who wear pink suits to football games, and he is on the edge of termination. Kirk Cameron, an actor, stated the biblical point of view against homosexuality and the media has posted comments made against the actor. Wait a minute! He made statements that align with the scriptures; words in the thousands of years-old Bible that has provided a moral guide for many civilizations.

Clearly, this has gone too far and now I have the answer for churches who want to welcome homosexuals but manage their authority in the church. At first glance, the statement "manage their authority" may seem awkward. I have felt a tremendous need to keep homosexuals within the arc of safety in salvation in Christ without pushing them away. And at the same time, I know how dynamic and powerful their testimony can be and it can be so demonstrative that they will always have a strong presence of leadership among saints who are at different levels of Christian understanding. Homosexuals seeking to grow spiritually will come to Christ with a contrite heart and will seek forgiveness and repent. The result will be defined between the person and God.

But some homosexuals, as is always with some sinners, will proclaim rightness in their sinful position to have same-sex relationships without spiritual conviction. The government is trying to push the change in church by-laws to state marriage is between two people instead of specifically stating "man and woman."

Some drinkers keep getting drunk, some liars lie more; and some fornicators and adulterers prey upon the members of the church. And I cannot accept the fact that God has not convicted them partially of their wrong.

A married heterosexual woman may have uncharacteristically wild, freaky, marital sex and question whether it was right to do what was done behind the sanctity of her bedroom walls. Yes, I recall moments with a cross around my neck in which I knew that the sex I had just partaken of with a female was so unrestrained that it should have been saved for marriage, or never done. So, how can these once-considered perverse, same-sex, generationally-immoral acts escape conscience- or spirit-driven scrutiny and judgment?

I cannot believe that some trepidation and conviction is not felt in the hearts of most in the LBGT community. I believe that the majority are waiting to see what happens, while demanding forgiveness. It is the church's role to offer correction and prayer through the Spirit of God. It would be just as ungodly and spiritually irresponsible to allow rebellious sinners to reign while never being told that they are going against the will of God and breaking religious doctrine.

Therefore, homosexuals who feel as if their conduct is not

under scrutiny by God and they want to be accepted as they are, they should attend regular churches until they get convicted by the Spirit to change. Those who will not change will seek to establish their own churches and church conventions. They will in effect become 'gay churches' and it is the belief of the faithful that God will take care of the rest. If they grow, it is similar to the sin in the world; for a season.

The same-gender referendum has passed in the state of Maryland and same-sex marriages will be allowed the first of the year, 2013.

April 30, 2013

Pro basketball player, Jason Collins has announced that he is gay and many questions have arisen. He is about seven-feet tall and the twin of Jarron Collins who also plays professional basketball. Jarron didn't know that his twin was gay and neither did his fiancée of eight years. Jason had no team at the time of his resignation but he has now landed with the Brooklyn Nets. He has been playing for more than 12 years professionally. The side story to all of this is that ESPN Sports commentator Chris Broussard spoke against the coming out party based on his Christian values. Jason was clear in proclaiming his Christian beliefs. Mr. Broussard could have been a little more gentle and touted the bravery of the young man (bravery?) and accepted his coming out as an opportunity for the player to develop an understanding about correcting improper sexual behavior; especially, since confession must come first prior to being forgiven. Now, Jason was engaged to a young lady for eight years and he must have done a great job of pretending because she expected him to be the father of her children. She is a tall, attractive female who now feels betrayed. Jason's mind had to focus on the attractiveness of his woman in order to keep her around. That's a whole lot of involved pretending. It confirms for me that sexual gratification is a choice; centered in the mind. So, what's the noise about when I say he needs to make better choices?

Every time an issue comes up that clearly identifies homosexuality as a choice, a wave of negative media arises to proclaim it as not being able to be changed.

Cynthia Nixon of the television show, *Sex and the City*, confirmed the choice aspect of sexuality when she stated that she didn't feel changed at all after being in a relationship with a man for 15 years and bearing two wonderful children; and then entering into a lesbian relationship and marriage with a woman. Gay advocates were upset when she refused to deny her previous heterosexual love as a mistake.

Any person leaving a heterosexual relationship for a same-sex relationship must surely prompt the person left alone to question whether or not displayed affections were real and at what point did it stop being authentic. Cynthia Nixon showed consideration and respect for the emotions, experiences, and children she shared with her husband of fifteen years. If you can change from heterosexual to homosexual, why can't one change from homosexual to heterosexual?

The Pope in Rio De Janeiro, Brazil
July 29, 2013

Pope Francis attended World Youth Day in Rio De Janeiro and spoke with compassion and sincerity that revealed the inclusive spiritual leadership of his office. He went on record as saying: "Who am I to judge a gay person?" when asked about any priest who was not sexually active but had come out as gay. The pope addressed the situation with love, mercy, and commonsense. Gay priests can still "search" for the Lord and show love and respect for others. In their search, prayerfully, they will come to the understanding that their leadership affects others who may think that they have found enough of God and being gay is fine with them. It is what the pope

163

does not say that allows one to interpret it as I just stated. Gay advocates rejoice with definitive and vague comments made by leaders that can be interpreted as pro-gay. Clearly, religious leaders speak with caution about the issue because they don't want to bear the burden of being called homophobic. The smallest declaration of what is in the Bible concerning sexual lifestyles apparently runs the risk of turning people away from organized religion; and that is contrary to going out into the world and saving souls. Christians who read the Bible read what it says and believe it to be the word of God addressing with clarity, homosexuality. As believers should, the pope supports people and the spiritual awareness that God can change anybody at any time.

The church dilemma still revolves around not marginalizing gay people while not supporting homosexuality. Christians for many years have said, "Love the sinner and hate the sin." We can separate the two but gay advocates don't want us to distinguish between the act and the person. My relatives love to drink and gamble and some go to church. I love them but they are sinning. According to the Bible, homosexuality is a sin and if I start ignoring certain scriptures because society calls me names, society then becomes my standard for living and not God.

Sexual Relationships

Society has made an informal and formal commitment to heterosexuality since the beginning of time. The other sexual appetites have been exceptions and when the need came to explain them, they were referenced as abnormal or strange. Now, with such a fair society springing up, we must understand that this sexual transition in which homosexuality, bisexuality, and the transgender insist upon being considered as normal elements of society, we must somehow indoctrinate the children; or teach them what to expect in a changing society.

In 2010, in Montana, a school district is facing the uproar of adding to the curriculum a proposed sex education program that teaches fifth-graders the different ways people have intercourse and first-graders about gay love. This controversy is a precursor to the debate in which the entire country will have to engage. And it may be for different reasons (such as bullying) but it will occur contrary to gay advocates.

As human sexuality develops, it impacts families, organizations, and every humanly conceived subject in the world. As sexuality has been engendered throughout society, the acceptance and promotion of the LBGT will proliferate through society as well. Society dictates what it wants to represent and how it should look.

Hundreds of years ago, American society decided that Africans were not welcome in the social structure except as slaves and laborers, and a few years ago they were not welcome to mingle socially with white members. In order to make this a reality laws had to be passed and schools had to be separate and specific interracial public interactions had to be outlawed. Entertainment venues were in compliance with the laws; as were advertising, and careers. The rules of separation were stated and implied to such a degree that places of worship, friendships, casual interactions, public restrooms and water fountains were all impacted. The laws were racist and degrading but formal and informal structures developed as a result of these laws.

Take the African-American experience and start from the end. Advertising, entertainment venues, and schools will reflect the new open LBGT experience. Gay lovers (husbands and wives?) will visit their spouses at school and hug and kiss and be introduced to the class. Commercials on television will openly push the gay agenda because of capitalism and it will be a new niche market in the United States and who will pay for this movement? The children will pay. Parents and grandparents, neighbors and friends will have conflict over what to believe and teach; and the children will have greater internal and physical conflicts.

But they will have the wonderful choice to now have sex with males and females; just as some people are pushing women to kiss other women saying it doesn't mean they are gay. Soon it will be Mommy had two lesbian lovers and Daddy had three gay lovers in college. We all will pay in ways that we cannot yet imagine. And it isn't homophobia because the facts speak for themselves. We don't teach anything about sexuality for children until late in middle school; and what we teach is more biological and scientific than socio-sexual. But there are no biological/scientific equivalents for homosexual loving. We will in effect teach children that they have a choice; to the majority of children who naturally choose heterosexuality.

Understand that we need to teach tolerance but we don't need to teach children that they have a choice of sexual orientations because some will take advantage of the right to choose simply because it is there. The proper attitude to take for society is to have no problem with what people choose to do in their personal lives but teaching a lifestyle as an option for children who cannot discern between nature and choice is propagating confusion.

The issue is greater than individual rights because the LBGT community has individual rights that should not be denied in such a free country as the USA. But the question remains: how do we want our society to look and what do we want to represent in the world? Where do the rights of conservative society end and individual rights begin? The church and other institutions are being forced to accept policies that are against Christian doctrine; therefore, against God (that's what we believe).

One church had a disagreement with its Baptist Convention because it refused to display the photos of same-sex couples in their journals. Well, here goes that good old Christian church again and they decided to compromise and have group photos only. Well, the church decided to leave the convention stating that it does not want to be a part of any organization that is not fair to all. Now, people who are caught up in the individual rights thing understand why the church pulled out of the convention but I want you to understand the other side.

Christians and Christian organizations are not supposed to support anything that is sinful; and yes, Christians believe that homosexuality is a sin. A sin is a willingness to go against the will of God. In the eyes of God, no one sin has precedence over another but in the eyes of humanity we know that things are different. Murder and sexual immorality rank high in what we refuse to promote or sponsor. Homosexuals may consider their families and lovers or spouses as wonderful additions to their lives and we are glad for some to have a semblance of what they consider as happiness; but we believe that true happiness comes with a relationship with Jesus Christ and that relationship will convict you and change you.

I constantly hear everyone bandy about the phrase of being born that way (homosexual) but they have not really determined that an extra chromosome makes you think and act gay. You choose your sexual partner based on a great range of variables, including impulse, thought, and environment. This choice has been evident in the number of homosexuals who have chosen to live as heterosexuals, only to change their minds and come out of the closet after marrying and having children. They chose to live as heterosexuals and they did a convincing job of it. People had pleasure and took pictures and had romantic outings for years; supposedly under the pretense of being heterosexual.

Society and the government can support same-sex marriage and relationships but the church will still bear the godly responsibility of restating what we believe God desires for the salvation of the soul. For many, religious convention is the umbrella that covers all institutions and the glue that holds the together while making sense of it all.

Doesn't society have a right to choose what it wants society to look like in the future? The answer is yes. Hundreds of years ago, this question could have been used to support slavery but what was the sleazy result of asking the question without addressing long-term consequences? Society refused to see the dilemma being played out among slavery that revealed the error of their ways.

I know, it can be considered as insensitive and it is easy for me to say, but I believe in the biblical perspective as practical and godly. I believe in godly, biblical precedence over individual rights. Matthew 19:4, Leviticus 18:22 and 20:13; and Romans 1:27 all make some reference to the godly version of marriage.

In a matter of asceticism, Christians deny or are prompted to refuse to engage in premarital sex (and ongoing worldly pleasures). Fornication is considered sin. Sex with the same gender is considered sin. In the interpretation of the Bible, we can contend about revenge (eye for an eye), female leadership, war (thou shall not kill), etc. But the issue of sex with the same gender is clearly spoken against and there is no debate for Christians who are not secularly influenced that homosexuality is a sin.

We are not to reject homosexuals but we are to encourage their relationship with Jesus Christ, believing that he only is capable of healing all of our sin-sick souls. We are encouraged to accept those who come just as they are but we don't have to post their lifestyles in our church bulletins and we don't have to allow them to become church leaders. Remember, the church leader issue is only because they have refused to admit their lives as being sinful; they profess a normalcy about a church-defined issue. It is heresy, so how can they become leaders unless churches declare the Bible is in error.

Society now almost declares it as a crime against humanity to call homosexuals sinners. But our faith declares it as such and we are all sinners; people who do something wrong that needs to be corrected. We don't run them away but the conviction of the soul often runs people away; just like saying adulterers are sinners and they don't want to hear it because they don't plan on ending the affair. The modern day contention is that a homosexual is born with a different sexual preference so it is something that cannot be corrected and neither should they desire to change. Sounds familiar to us Christians: people enjoy sin so much that they question biblical doctrine and its interpretations when it speaks against their pleasures. The birth of a baby hooked on drugs or alcohol does not negate the fact that it needs to be made clean. The sinner is born immoral and capable of doing anything that goes against the will of God. Salvation through Jesus Christ offers the sinner the empowerment to change beyond his or her own lack of will power. Yes, the temptation is to say I want to change some things and not others. Yes, the temptation is to get people within spiritual circles to accept my sin as 'regular.' But the Spirit of God declares that which is unrighteous and we know (whether we admit it or not) what goes against God's will.

Now, having said all that, it is not a Christian's job to speak against the homosexual but to speak up for having a relationship with Christ. We know that a change occurred in us due to our faith and obedience. Our goal is to accept the sinner in church and watch God do the rest. But the sinner cannot come to church and dictate to the church what doctrine is outdated or should be changed. For instance, female leadership is still a debated and contested issue in modern churches. It is easy to align two groups to contest the church under the guise of moving it into the 21st century, and the resulting confusion simply diverts the subject of sin even more.

It is truly amazing to me that a coalition of ministers in Washington, D. C. have joined forces in marrying homosexuals. They have ignored the declaration of homosexuality as sin and moved to marry or validate the sin under the dark veil of spiritual misinterpretation and meeting the requests of the people. In dealing with this monumental topic in a reasonable manner, we would assume that many theologians would come together; reveal interpretations; debate and contest; and initiate a progressive methodology for change; if change is needed. But this is beyond reasoning because every Christian supposedly believes that the Bible is the humanly inspired word of God; so, popularity or social compromise have nothing to do with biblical obedience. Change based solely on societal impulses and the rights of chosen lifestyles cannot affect true believers---well, it's not supposed to make us reinterpret the scriptures.

The greatest fault that I perceive is found in the desire to go against the will of God. When I basked in the aroma of sin, I fixed things in my mind to say that my sin was not offensive to God. Some sins, I actually reasoned to be performing a good deed. Yes, a kind man who offered love to the forlorn and comfort to those who comforted me. I reasoned that church could be in the heart and not needed to inconvenience me by pulling me out of my bed after a rough, late Saturday night creeping into early Sunday morning.

Lastly, society has the right to determine what rights may negatively impact the familial and sexual structure of its subgroups; and through the ages, theologians have assisted in such thinking. I know that this is the same argument that was used to justify slavery but that doesn't mean that the fundamental principle of the argument is wrong because it was wrongly applied. Remember, nothing is done in a vacuum: children will be encouraged to accept the choices of children who have not even developed a sense of sexuality in most cases; and teens will be encouraged to have various choices when going through those intense, hormonal years. And just like now; some say a little kissing among females doesn't make a girl a lesbian. What about a little kissing among boys?

For many, the sexual impulse is all that matters; especially, in adolescence. Men will meet women who have had a variety of sexual experiences; and we have problems now trusting each other so what happens when the number of potential suitors, fornicators, and adulterers increases two-fold, and crosses gender? Suddenly, we can clearly see that it is a choice except for cases of biological "missteps." It is my personal belief that sexual preferences are still choices; and among these choices, impulses abound for a variety of reasons. Unadulterated individual freedoms must not override society's right to structure certain aspects of its moral code; in spite of the fact that society has abused this right in the past.

Leviticus 18:22 and 20:13 are also debated among denominations and scholars.

Leviticus 18:22 - " *Thou shalt not lie with mankind, as with womankind: it is abomination."*

Leviticus 20:13 - *"If a man also lie with mankind, as he lieth with a woman, both of them have committed an abomination: they shall surely be put to death; their blood shall be upon them."*

1 Corinthians 6:9-10 –" Know ye not that the unrighteous shall not inherit the kingdom of God? Be not deceived: neither fornicators, nor idolaters, nor adulterers, nor effeminate, nor abusers of themselves with mankind, [10] Nor thieves, nor covetous, nor drunkards, nor revilers, nor extortioners, shall inherit the kingdom of God."

To the layperson and to the intolerant, these words may mean that the aforementioned are not going to heaven. Hence, a little boy got a standing ovation in church when he sang "Aint No Homos Gonna Make it to Heaven." In the secular vein, people are outraged and rightfully consider this as a homophobic statement.

In the spiritual context, sexuality is not an issue in heaven...sex is not the ultimate sin; but an ever-improving relationship with God is our goal. A layperson could also interpret this as saying that acceptance of Christ is transforming so in living under God's grace, we do wrong and see it as wrong with no excuses. Admission of our wrongs and not persuading others to do wrong is a part of the transformation. This is for any sin. So, invariably, those of us who have been transformed from drug-addictions, sexual promiscuity and other sexual sins, gambling and other addictions; know that everyone doesn't get to the point where they can see their sins as sins.

One of the most difficult things to do in an individual's early growth in Christianity is to recognize a favorite sin as sin without any excuses or exceptions (I only do this sin once every two weeks). Homosexuals entering the church may proclaim that they were born that way and that to aligns with Christian thought: "...born into sin, shaped in iniquity." All humans, especially those with a transformed mind in Christ, have the ability to choose the path away from sin.

While the scripture may sound clear, the debate actually centers on the use of the Greek word that this particular version of the Bible translates as "homosexual offenders." The term is "arsenokoite."

Some say that it is a reference to male prostitutes rather than to two committed homosexuals. Yet, others argue that Paul, who wrote the passage, would not have repeated "male prostitutes" twice. Even others argue that the two root words in arsenokoite are the same terms used to prohibit any premarital or extramarital sexual relations, so they may not refer to homosexual relations alone.

Again, you can try to interpret the word above to suit whatever stance you desire but the bottom line is the following scripture declares it as sin but there is a way to get into heaven.

1 Corinthians 6:11 - "And that is what some of you were. But you were washed, you were sanctified, you were justified in the name of the Lord Jesus Christ and by the Spirit of our God."

Now having said all of this, it really matters not what labels we give people based on their sins, or what labels they give themselves. Christians believe it is the word of God that transforms. People come to church as they are and we really should not label them even if they want to be labeled. We should not categorize their sins even if they want it categorized. The issue in church is not to wear my sexuality as a badge or as a possible distraction but to praise God, ingest the word; and pray for relationships; especially the one with Jesus Christ.

Excerpts from Internet Article by Kelli Mahoney. Christian Teen Guide. About.com, Christian Teens

Heterosexuals

When I was young, I saw the movie, The Other side of

Midnight, and I knew that we were all going to hell in a hand-basket. I heard profanity and viewed some almost nude scenes, and I predicted that soon they would say anything they wanted on television and do whatever they wanted; all in the name of entertainment. But at the same time, I wondered on what channel did that almost-naked woman appear; and I searched for it. The dilemma was exposed: when I seek to do right, evil is present to entice me to do wrong. We spend most of our lives trying to capture that sexual mystique and passion that we discovered when the hormones initially raged in our bodies. We dreamed it; our music commanded our souls about it; we went to school to be around it; and presently, we spend undisclosed amounts of money to work our vision of it.

Moral, religious principles help to gather us in as a society, when we go too far or want to go too far. But society speaks loudly when it comes to sex and this young country wants everyone's rights to be observed. Have sex with any consenting adult and worry about disease and babies later. Society will somehow manage to pay for it all. Of course, being a capitalistic society, jobs are ensured and salaries are paid. Even prisons get a chance to promote homosexuality and increased disease. There may be a connection with the increase of AIDS among HAMS (heterosexual American Soul males) due to the large percentages that are locked up. Do they use condoms in prison?

Babies and diseases keep Democratic programs self-perpetuating; and people have jobs.

Immigration

Immigration had not been a problem for early America. The country simply discriminated. Africans in the country were allowed to stay here but periodically they were encouraged to go back to Africa although by the early 1900's most were born in this country. Mainly, white people were allowed to come into the country; and a few other people of color.

The Great Melting Pot that is the USA is finding it difficult to merge the customs and ideologies of all people.

While promoting her movie 'The Switch' earlier this week, Jennifer Aniston told reporters that women don't need men to start a family or be good mothers. When Bill O'Reilly caught wind of her statement, he debated the topic of single motherhood on 'The O'Reilly Factor' and called out the 41-year-old actress.

Capitalism and Social Structure

As a result of trying to achieve more income, we leave our children at home with strangers while we leave the home to earn a living. African Americans had simple lives, no money and the hope of the future was placed in the children. My grandmother lived behind me and at least two uncles and one aunt lived within two-hundred yards of her. Children were often shouldered with the responsibility to be the best. Capitalistic society which was the foundation of slavery, now breeds a new slave-type: the worker who has no generations to model success so they go into the world excited about new ventures and failing to prepare. They have prepared for game systems and video music; and fashionable attire but they have no glue that we are expecting their return within six months; hopefully having no babies, no diseases, and particularly, alive.

Effectively, America established a social caste system with the freeing of slaves and little or no economic assistance. We were the first Mexicans because we would do anything to escape the sharecropper system that was rigged to keep people in debt and impoverished. With freedom, people wanted to express themselves and venture into the North were it has always been rumored to be better. This action or Diaspora effectively chopped the nuclear family's legs off at the knees. Immigrants to America, including the Mexicans, have many families living in the same house. This strategy allows the families to accumulate some financial foundation prior to leaving the home and striking out on their own.

Human interaction, especially capitalism in America, always depends on generalities, no matter how ill=conceived. We think that many Italians are gangsters, Chinese immigrants can cook well; Jews are economically frugal; and on it goes. Racism was so rancid in America that AMS had many stereotypes yet we were the ones dealt an injustice. Lazy? That's a lie because we built the country along with some Chinese people working on the railroads. Liars? That may have been true because we lied all day long to survive. It took a skilled liar to convince the master that he was happy and not even thinking about escaping to freedom somewhere. We lied about reading because it wasn't allowed; and lied about how much we loved the little children of our oppressors. That's right. Our wives and mothers were raped, and told to take care of the master's children; and we talked about bighead ugly babies even if it wasn't true.

Having no experience with starting a culture, and having everyone coming from different tribes, everyone went their own separate ways; not knowing that we were officially recognized as one culture: black. This was the time to do the immigrant thing and live in one house and teach finances, and saving but we had no one to teach us collectively because we were freed to be society's social, economic, and emotional scavengers.

A Caucasian male taught my father real estate investing in the forties but none of us wanted to do that. We chose to leave the South and venture into a world of opportunities. Some AMS had talent and they made it on their talent. Some had financial training or the sense to save and they prospered. We looked good individually and still do. But the greatest threat to the culture of AMS is financial scurvy. We attain much but we marry other races and get divorced and the other races are blessed. We spend more than any other race but we make no demands of those with whom we spend our dollars.

It was a law in some places that AMS and Caucasians could not mix or marry. That just made the apple more appealing. Such anti-miscegenation laws actually foreshadowed a method of growing a culture that had yet to be defined. A rule that no young AMS superstars (athletes or intellectuals) could marry white girls would have increased AMS familial economic growth; at least in Boston. All other brothers who wanted to could and of course, if you were a late bloomer and doing nothing much (a struggling actor) and suddenly you blew up, we would understand. There are plenty of AMS women of light-skin and of a culturally different nature to appease the fleshy desires of these brothers. We want the money from your first divorce to remain in the community. Your second wife could be whatever race you desired.

Guidance

Some people look at bad luck as some power over life but faith teaches that there is no such thing. But we are in spiritual warfare so bad things may signal a need for spiritual power. If I want to claim the victory against evil, the person suffering bad luck must dedicate a part of life to praying and studying God's word.

Personal Tragedy

We often do things and reflect upon them as we get older. It is difficult to understand how a woman gets an abortion in order to avoid taking care of a baby; but an abortion means that she is not killing a baby but an embryo. Humanity can reason various viewpoints but the underlying fact is taking a life that if left alone would grow into a person. The immense guilt felt in those latter years has to frequently become overwhelming.

When I was diagnosed with cancer (Hodgkins Lymphoma), I initially thought about the relationship that I had with God that was established by my parents. But it was the first time that I considered the relationship. I had taken it for granted up to thirty-one years of age. I now had to know if God was real and if he would consider saving me from death in spite of my past neglect of him. After all, I had been adopted at birth and given to my great-uncle and great-aunt. I could have been aborted; and surely it came across someone's mind.

It was a rough transition to start reading the Bible after so many years; and it was not easy to go to church on a regular basis at first. I began to say my prayers again but the intensity and regularity were inconsistent due to a lack of faith and an overwhelming since of guilt.

I knew that I deserved to die and although I began to speak death to myself and to others around me, I realized that I could not wait for death. I prayed about the guilt and my poor marital efforts; and my sole potential as a secular dad. One day something intense like this will occur in their lives and they will also need to have a relationship with God that is viable and results-oriented. I thought, what a good thing to already have a relationship in place after those teenage years; those times when we are filled with so many choices that we consistently and intentionally made a few poor ones thinking that it was okay.

But the soul has to pay. The poor choices eventually testified to the soul that my personal God was okay with sin; with me doing whatever I wanted to do as long as I respected him. Respect for God came in the form of many things that did not interfere with my chosen lifestyle: I said grace at the table to myself if I was not with a lot of sinners. I said thank you Jesus when I barely avoided car accidents. I prayed with my wife ever so often. We taught our children "The Lord's Prayer." I stopped cursing and drinking alcoholic beverages.

It wasn't really showing respect. I was trying to deceive God into believing that I loved him. While he was hugging me and showing me love, I kept him as a part-time lover, pushing him away while only wanting to occasionally hold his hand. You would think that I had to know that he knew all about me, especially since he was God. But no lightning bolts and no train wrecks and no great disasters, testified to me that our relationship was still fine in the lukewarm mode. The soul had to pay. I paid indeed and the brute force of the ordeal prompted me to challenge God and he accepted the challenge. This put the onus of faith right back in my court and I followed suite with my faith in him.

Education

In 2010, less than half (47%) of African American males are graduating from high school; and when you list the specifics in many

177

cities, it is far worse than one could ever imagine. In the midst of all of this data, the Baltimore City Public School System wants to be the first to implement merit pay for teachers. It is another American smoke screen, devised to take the focus off the immense scope of the problem and proclaim a faux resolution that will merely allow people to systematically conclude that firing and hiring new teachers will resolve the problem.

The smokescreen will also allow the archaic school systems across the nation to take the focus off poor student performance and parental lack and put it on to a capitalistic issue---money.

The truth is that education in America is a capitalistic issue. Of course, no one can take the blame for the wide array of variables impacting student performance. But teachers grade papers, adhere to quarterly and yearly new standards, provide after-school tutoring, and do extensive lesson planning for various student learning styles and levels. All of this while meeting the extra demands by principals outside of contractual obligations; due to fear of retaliation on annual evaluations.

Recent contract negotiations proclaim a student achievement-based system combined with merit pay. Recent hard economic times have made teachers desperate for small things like 2% raises. The spiel is, if we take the small raises with some dangling carrot cash ($1750) just before the holidays; we will then accept the merit pay system that accompanies such benefits.

Surprisingly, teachers voted for it with the full-support of union leaders; and in 2013 we can see what we accepted in a clearer, unbiased light. The evaluation process had not been completed so management had the opportunity to add/develop evaluation tools that would not be accepted if put in contract negotiations prior to voting. In effect, our system of evaluation increased in minutia to the point that it would take perfect human beings to attain the highest ratings. Or teachers who have attained the favor of principals.

The issue of firing teachers becomes more of an consequential-performance issue that will automatically come into play because teachers, students, schools, and systems have bad or low-performing years. After a year of unsatisfactory evaluations, administrators get to reduce the payroll. Of course, the new teacher will have even less support and the turnover for such teachers is high so administrators will need to be cautious about who gets picked for termination. Yes, picked for termination. New teachers have less support but they usually do as they are told and they don't impact the budget as much. The inefficiency of the system is so high that any teacher at any given time can fail to meet the requirements and be terminated.

Once our school system negotiates the ability to fire teachers based on student achievement; they will encourage administrators to reduce their individual payrolls due to the school not making Annual Yearly Progress. A school cannot have an abundance of proficient teachers with poor test scores because the problem would then be attributable to the administrators. The reasons will be legitimate but enforcement will be highly subjective as most inner-city teachers teach in volatile environments where dysfunctional families; transient communities; gangs infesting middle and high schools; drug-addicted parents and pedophiles; as well as the usual social ills of poverty and single-parent homes, reign. What's a good or good-enough-teacher to do when you get the class that has scored the lowest from first grade to fifth grade and every teacher has received a bad evaluation? Now it is your turn, sixth grade teacher. But of course, in this economic downturn, the brilliant school superintendent will use a corporate strategy that will indeed lower the payroll and put younger, less tenured teachers at the helm. They probably envision the increase in new teachers entering the system will offset the dynamic impact of veteran teachers being terminated. I don't think it will be as easy as he or she thinks because everyone isn't cut out to teach in urban environments; and turnover is highest (I'm sure) among new teachers with one- to three-years-experience.

Kelly-Williams-Bolar lives in a housing project in Akron, Ohio. She wanted to obtain a better education for her two daughters so she used the address of her father to enable her to send her daughters to school in the better area. The mother of two is being sent to jail for this heinous crime.

Besides being a single mom, Williams-Bolar was going to school part time in the hope of getting a job as a teacher. The judge noted that because Williams-Bolar has been convicted of a felony, she will no longer be allowed to teach in the state of Ohio. Therefore, the punishment that she and her girls will face is set to last a lifetime.

What is a caring, struggling parent to do? In one school system, the leaders proclaim the achievement of reducing suspensions by almost fifty-percent. At first glance, this is a wonderful accomplishment. Children cannot learn if they are suspended. Federal dollars cannot flow if many of these students are special education students with IEPs; and with school systems needing so much money, it makes good business sense. But the practical application of keeping unruly, misbehaved, uninterested students in class with other students is unmanageable. First, it is a difficult process to manage borderline bad behavior when you can't suspend students. Throw in the variable of students who take advantage of such a system and it becomes obvious to other students who has the power in the classroom. Without a buy-in from students to participate and not disrupt, student behavior in any classroom will disrupt learning.

The worst part is that this phenomenon is occurring in urban environments. A few varied minorities and some Caucasians are suffering because academically, we cannot sustain this house of cards as each year another group of students learns what the system will not do and what they are empowered to do.

May 8, 2010

The local and national news became focused on a child four or five years of age, who had been suspended from school. They showed a psychologist who spoke against the suspension because of the damage to the child. The poor mother had lost her job because of the numerous times she had to report to the school due to the boy's behavior. And each time the boy was suspended, she had to attend a mandatory reinstatement meeting. I think he had been suspended 12-15 times in the 2011-2012 school year.

Society refuses to address the question that all teachers and many parents want answered: what in the world are you supposed to do with these type of children. Yes, they have been diagnosed with a learning disability and ADD and ADHD; but we still need to protect other students and establish a decent learning environment. One child that refuses to accept the boundaries established for the sake of learning, negatively impacts the classroom; influences borderline, similar behaviors in other students; and reaffirms the powerlessness of the teacher in stopping a physically, off-task child. We are not supposed to yell at them but they yell and curse at us. We are not supposed to touch, grab, or hit them, yet they can hit us. If you suspend a child, it keeps the child from learning but that same child may have eradicated days or weeks of learning with his or her behavior.

Jan. 23, 2012

Excerpts from an article by Trymaine Lee, reporter

People in Texas are still trying to make us pay for the atrocities suffered by us. Huh? An ultra-conservative school board in Texas sought to change its school textbooks to lighten the barbarism and negativism of slavery. Yes, it becomes difficult to tell children that an entire race of people were enslaved, physically and sexually-abused, all for the sake of capitalism in America. Ummm. How can we change that so that our white children don't grow up ashamed of their ancestors history in a society growing in multi-culturism and sympathy for other ethnicities? I know. Let's rewrite the history books so no one will know about the atrocities. Now "a group of Tea Party activists in Tennessee has renewed its push to whitewash school textbooks." They are working on removing references to slavery from the books; as well as statements connecting the country's founders as having owned slaves.

Mr. Lee reports that Hal Rounds, the Fayette County attorney and spokesman for the group, seeks to rewrite history so as to avoid criticism of the founders of this country. I surmise that same logic is the reason some people say the Holocaust never happened. But it did happen; and it explains a great deal of the Jewish trek through oppression and perseverance. This country needs to know how it became a country: free land stolen from the Native Americans was cultivated by free labor from African slaves.

Mr. Lee reports Hal Rounds as saying (according to The Commercial Appeal), "The thing we need to focus on about the founders is that, given the social structure of their time, they were revolutionaries who brought liberty into a world where it hadn't existed, to everybody -- not all equally instantly -- and it was their progress that we need to look at." This is what my AMS ears hear: Yes, we, the former oppressors, strongly desire to have our sins washed away; and since we have control over the majority opinion right now, let's ignore some aspects of history and change others to lessen the brutal imagery of slavery.

The Texas Board of Education is moving rapidly ahead and has already changed/ revised its social studies curriculum so as to "put a conservative twist on history through revised textbooks and teaching standards." It would be nice if we could simply erase the actions of devious groups by changing history but we cannot. Hitler killed millions of people to further a socio-political agenda; and we should never forget it because another fool could come along and try the same thing. Some people would stand around and listen to the fool because they would never believe that it could become that extreme a situation. Well, America stole land and enslaved people for immense profit and free labor. A large segment of AMERICA has roots and ties to the institution; we are not supposed to whitewash it and we don't want to. Stop adding insult to injury for African-Americans by erasing the great historical trials that we have overcome.

As reported by Mr. Lee, these revisions seek to have children explore the positive aspects of "American slavery, lifting the stature of Jefferson S. Davis to that of Abraham Lincoln..." Okay. I think that is enough. Remind me to ask a lot of questions the next time I travel to Texas. Thank God, these ultraconservative, racist actions failed to pass.

Mr. Lee gives us a warning of sorts: "The influence of the amended textbooks will likely reach far beyond the state of Texas. The state is one of the largest purchasers of textbooks, and many other states adopt Texas's books and standards."

Newtown Sandy Hook Elementary Shootings

A deranged young killer broke into Sandy Hook Elementary School and killed twenty children and six adults. It was an abominable, terroristic act which has finally led to discussions regarding security issues in our schools and, most importantly, overall gun control.

The issue regarding gun rights or the Second Amendment Right to bear arms is a right guaranteed by our great constitution. The fact is: do we really need it, and at what cost? For revolution, the government has that covered because no one group is powerful enough to overthrow the government. If you side with a warring faction against the government, you are better off without weapons (civil disobedience) because your other guaranteed rights will protect you.

What about foreign invasions? Again, we have poured our tax dollars into the military and we are covered on that aspect as well. The only reasoning for gun ownership is hunting and sport. The smallish, powerful handguns and the larger extremely powerful assault rifles have no place in either. In the AMS communities, the handguns have a devastating impact on our youth whose lives are often snatched by the illicit profession of selling illegal drugs. The handguns seem powerful and manly but their sell and use cannot compare to the loss of so many lives. Sadly, the Newtown killing of so many white children may alert the nation to the dangers of these weapons that many in my community have been warning about for decades; but the NRA and its dollars have a more powerful voice in America.

Lisa Wade, professor of sociology at Occidental College, wrote a thought-provoking article, "Sociological Images" in 2010.

Dr. Wade compares the responses of the media and society to two 7-year olds who took joyrides in the family vehicles. In her article is a link to a "Today" show segment that covers a white boy who took his family's car and got caught by police. The white child is interviewed with his family. His father describes the event rather lightheartedly and Merideth Viera asks questions with a tone of talking to a 7-year old boy. She speaks with understanding and with the intent to ensure that the boy knows the error of his ways. When the questioning may implicate the boy as a social deviate, his parents intervene to explain how his childish mind was working; ensuring a specific image displayed to the public about the child and the parents.

Dr. Wade describes it as a "heartwarming, human interest story with a happy ending. The child is framed as a fundamentally good kid who was curious and perhaps a bit impetuous."

The AMS 7-year old does not have any adult participating in the interview with him and coverage by CNN tends to differ from coverage by the "Today" show.

He, took the family car for a joyride and was interviewed without adult supervision so his honesty was self-deprecating and revealing; confirming social stereotypes and fears. But these same fears could have been revealed in the conversation with the other seven year old had his parents not been present to filter his responses.

Dr. Wade points out that the black boy's story is filmed on the street. He is slyly presented as the "criminal in the making." She points out the nuances of the framing of the story. "With an absolutely polar introduction of "Not your typical 7-year-old," this story is filmed in the criminal's traditional environment; on the streets.

The interviewer, without adult supervision and guidance, asks Latarian why he took the car. The boy replied honestly but unwisely, as a child is prone to do: "I wanted to do it 'cause it's fun, it's fun to do bad things." The boy further stated, "...I wanted to do hoodrat stuff with my friends."

Dr. Wade reveals that a longer version of the story "focuses on a reporter who explains that the police plan to go forward with charges of grand theft against him." The police officers know that he is too young to be arrested but they want to get him "into the system, so that they can get him some type of help."

I would argue that it is this same predetermined mindset of AMS as hardcore criminals that helped to prevent the conviction of the killer of Trayvon Miller. Dr. Wade reminds us that both boys are 7 year-old children but they are being treated so differently that the treatment impacts the children's view of themselves. In the case of the AMS child, police paperwork and his environment prepares him for a deviant lifestyle.

American Politics

AMS has enjoyed the two-party system in America. The Republican Party of the early years of this republic was filled with responsible activists who wanted to abolish slavery; they represented principles and ideologies similar to the Democratic Party today. The party also supported civil rights through the 1950's. and then something happened.

Such political landscape changes remind us that there are kind, considerate people on both sides of the political fence.

Rep. Mo Brooks, R-Al., boldly states that Democrats are waging a war on whites. He feels that Barack Obama and the Democrats are dividing us "all on race, on sex, creed, envy, class warfare---all those kinds of things."

Rep. Brooks correctly points out the subject matter but he slyly omits who makes these issues viable by not addressing the current structure of politics in America. By not doing, by not working towards change in the subject matter (race, sex, creed, envy, class warfare) anyone who does address it can be perceived as fighting against the status quo which happens to favor Caucasians.

In North Carolina, as in other states where Republicans have substantial or majority power, they seek to turn back the hands of time by fighting against Medicaid and higher education funding; and changing election laws to adversely affect minority voting. Again, to be fair, there is another viewpoint saying the elderly must put in their fair share and even education must feel the pinch of tightening the American belt. But attempts to restrict voting can be perceived as anti-American.

Adverse legislation against minority voting can be perceived as an effort by one party to limit the number of potential voters who would vote against their ideologies. Hey, that's a new way of doing things (not). Since your party chooses not to adapt to the country's new direction, why not work tirelessly for changing election laws so that greater numbers of people who oppose your unchanging ways will not be able to vote.

Reverend William Barber II decided to do something about these intense efforts to restrict voting among minorities. He led a small group of clergy and activists into the state legislative building in Raleigh where they sang, quoted from the Bible, and blocked the doors to the legislative chambers. Well, Hallelujah! This event happened on the last Monday of April 2013.

Of course, the group was arrested but the story gets so much better. The following Monday a group of about 100 showed up to protest. And people continued to come and protest each of the following Mondays until the group grew into thousands. Copycat groups have organized in other southern states where GOP legislation seeks to turn back the clock on election laws. Thank you Rev. Barber and North Carolina because you pulled out some old activism methods that still have power in 2014 and beyond.

The Supreme Court ruled in favor of Shelby County and overturned a crucial section of the Voting Rights Act. In dissent, Justice Ruth Ginsburg stated that getting rid of the critical section was akin to "throwing away your umbrella in a rainstorm because you are not getting wet." So what is this crucial section and what's the big deal?

The 1965 law required that lawmakers in states with a history of discriminating against minority voters get federal permission before changing voting rules. The Supreme Court has changed the formula used to determine which jurisdictions are required to get federal permission for election changes. Well, that seems fair, doesn't it? Shelby County argued that with all of this great progress in the country, who needs these nasty old voting rights requirements to ensure that states (mainly southern) maintain equal and fair voting laws that will not restrict voters? The answer is those same racist, redneck areas of the country who want to get rid of them. Duh?

If so much progress had been made then why get rid of them; unless you want to do some of the things done in the good 'ole days to restrict voting among minorities and groups that will not vote a specific way. in the south, that specific way is Republican. Now, GOP lawmakers with Cheshire Cat grins are searching out stronghold states for opportunities to pass new voting restrictions. Yes, this is still America.

It should be wonderfully representative of a great republic to have a democratic system which offers alternatives for liberals when Democrats get too liberal and for conservatives when Republicans get too conservative. It has been a pleasure to enjoy watching budgetary policy based on one or two terms of party/governmental success; followed by a newly elected opposing party's correction. For instance, Democrats often provide big government to take care of the people in crucial times. Republicans control the excess by pulling the belt tighter; and this eventually provides an upswing in the economy. It has been quite pleasurable to watch the two party system until now; until the influence of the

Tea Party extremists upon the Republican party. Their racial and class issues are widely pushed through in the form of political beliefs. Of course, the Tea Party agenda would proclaim that they have poor people as well in their party so how can they have class issues. Their class issues are not among white folks but in keeping minorities from ascending from where America has pushed us.

November 05, 2012

This election campaign has been brutal. AMS are fighting on Christian programs about same-sex marriage in Maryland. The radio is bombarding the air waves with rhetoric concerning fairness and equality; while Christians address God's moral principles. Something just doesn't seem right with the whole thing. Seemingly, out of the blue, a Democratic governor endorsed same-sex marriage when the economy was going down the tubes in Maryland and across the country.

As a member of the AMS community, I reserve the right to smell conspiracy. It appeared to be some sort of distraction strategy because the need for and improved economy and jobs was a greater priority. We had visitors from other states including Rev. Al Sharpton, eagerly coming to Maryland just to advocate same-sex marriage.

I understood the significance of the issue for many people. Denying health and death benefits after living with someone as a couple. I understand that part. But here is the Reverend Al and the Reverend Delmont Coates speaking confidently against what is printed in the Bible; not subject to weird interpretations because it says what it says in a variety of places.

It appears that the black clergy of several large congregations are endorsing this same-sex marriage law which conflicts with the word of God. I am fair and I understand the dilemma because people want their gay relatives to be happy but as a sinner saved by grace I have always treaded with caution when advocating a stance against scriptures because usually it is my selfish, human desire and rationale.

By rule, believers need to be careful about contradicting God's word in an attempt to gain humanity's favor. This has to be confusing for those who are borderline potential converts; and reassuring to those who profess Christ but are still steeped in sin. This means that some scriptural guidance is debatable.

Black folks are so fair. Yes, President Obama has offended many and the country is in just as big a pickle as it was before he entered the White House. Yes, he has done some good things but far more needs to be done. He has been blocked on every side so the evaluation of his job is biased against him because he has had very little cooperation across the aisle.

I don't blame the Republicans for going against almost every idea, good and bad, that President and Team Obama present. The symbol of the Grand Old Party is a donkey. And that's not fair because at one time the Republicans favored civil rights issues and the Democrats were against such humane efforts. The Republican Party was organized in 1854 to fight the "Kansas-Nebraska Act, which threatened to extend slavery into the territories." The Republican Party was the party of AMS up to the Great Depression. In our two-party system, these guys are literally fighting for their jobs and the future of their party.

Imagine what the Obama presidency could do: more and more black and brown people could vie for the presidency and win. The pink, blue-eyed, champion of American society could become an outdated concept in this country's politics. So, fight they must. I just don't like the way of fighting about everything so much so that the government fails to serve the people.

The Mosque Near Ground Zero

I am only slightly concerned about the Islamic mosque or Islamic cultural center going up in downtown New York near Ground Zero. As Americans, they have the right to purchase property and serve the god of their choosing. That pretty much is the President's retort as well. As an American citizen, I can empathize with the angst of those who reject the idea. Isn't that just a bad idea: to be reminded of the religious zealots that caused 911 by establishing a mosque within one mile of Ground Zero? I am curious as to the thought processes of the person who suggested it and those who agreed to support it financially. Surely, someone in that meeting had to say, "I don't care what they have to say about it...it's my fortune and they made the rules."

We can say that there are good Muslims and that is correct. Good Muslims didn't perform the horrible act. But we are confused because bad people and neutral people engaged in the planning; and some 'good people' had foreknowledge about the horrific act.

Think about how many cousins and friends and siblings had to know what was happening but never did anything about it. Who draws the line in the sky that delineates good and bad Muslims? Isn't it simply war against the infidels and are all non-Islamic people infidels? That's the religion so bad Muslims and good Muslims believe the same thing but bad Muslims obediently engage in jihad. We shouldn't even think of it as religious fanaticism but it has been proclaimed as such by the group worldwide. If my religion has so many people misinterpreting verses as violence perhaps it is the religion that has some loopholes that need to be closed. But no one appears to be closing them. Islam is the religion of the zealots that caused 9/11 to be a day of infamy and heroism. It is the religion that seems to nurture extremists. Or it is the extremists who choose to use Islam as an excuse to commit violence?

In personal religious and familial matters, it is difficult to separate from the intrinsic emotions that nurture closeness and commitments; and who wants to? Family members lie for murderers and tell themselves that surely: "Bobo won't do it...he would never do such a thing...would he?" What happens when Bobo plans it and brings friends over and you disapprove? Now your life and your family's lives are in danger and you don't want to snitch on Bobo; although you know this to be the right thing to do. It is easier to tell yourself to pray, that the plan will not come to fruition; that Bobo is not really that evil...or is he?

What if the money used to purchase the property came from Muslim extremists? The guy who came up with the idea appeared on television and stated that he has insured that no monies were taken from such extremist groups. If I was among the Muslims who originally proposed the idea, I would have dropped this issue at the slightest conflict so as not to stir up suppressed feelings. Terrorist zealots are still blowing up places around the world. I believe in religious freedom, but some freedoms have to be limited. If this was a Muslim nation, and some crazy Christians flew planes into the Trade Center, the religion would be banned throughout the country and all followers might have their freedoms restricted or face execution.

But thank God for America. Here is where I have problems with the President. He could have simply remained silent on the issue. Or, he could have expressed: "Although, I believe in the right of all Americans to purchase property and build what they may, I empathize with the emotional conflict felt by the good citizens of New York and the country." I would have said: I love the Muslims; they are credited with getting many of my AMS brothers out of jail and setting them on a right path. But it seems as if a huge Muslim Cultural Center near Ground Zero might appear to be sneering at America and rubbing our faces in what some call victory, but we call cowardly, murderous attacks." In a sense, a religious building becomes a monument to Islamic fanaticism and violence; and to American freedoms coming to bite us in our ACLU posteriors.

I am going to be honest: I supported George Bush in going to war in the Middle East, initially. I didn't really care if he found WMD; I wanted the fanatics to know that the USA is still the toughest, butt-kicking country in the world and we will go and kick butt all over the world against anybody who attacks us in the comfort of our own powerful cities. I didn't think about these countries having their peace disturbed and the safety of their children jeopardized.

But I didn't plan on us staying over there for ten years either. I didn't think that my sons might get drafted to fight over there. I wanted us to send a message; hit it and come back home. Clinton bombed a few caves and came back too quickly. Bush did what needed to be done. Now, President Obama is doing what needs to be done in getting us out.

The status quo for Republican politics in 2012 was to advise black folks on welfare and pulling themselves up by their own bootstraps or tennis shoe laces. Amazingly, these erudite politicians don't understand that white folks have always been the majority on welfare and statistics on these tough economic times will accentuate this fact. So, why did Newt Gingrich and Rick Santorum consistently speak of blacks asking for welfare and handouts as a part of their platform during their ill-fated run for the Republican nomination for the Presidential election of 2012?

Every minority group needs a central group to take up their cause. For the issues in Texas, a representative group would send someone to the location and interview concerned parties. The central group would initiate a game plan to combat the evil. Someone to lead and gather information about the situation and then provide press releases through a common website and other forms of media. I like the website established by Dr. Boyce Watkins, Professor of Urban Studies, Syracuse University; and founder of YourBlackWorld.com.

Clearly, the new strategy that has been embraced by conservatives and the Tea Party, is to attack minority issues to galvanize support from the majority race; support based on the logic of needing fairness for white folks as well; especially in this economic downturn presided over by an African American. Another strategy is to create inconveniences in the voting process; advocating the ease of Voter ID laws. Ignite minority fears about showing their identification, make certain demands; and the word will spread about great intrusions and that it's not worth being a dedicated voter. Yes, the 15th Amendment guarantees against such obstructions to exercising our rights.

June 29, 2012

The solution proposed by Rick Perry, governor of Texas, and the Republican Party platform for 2012 is to repeal the Voting Rights Act. Let's not play any games by asking for extra identification, poll tax, and demanding that you urban people wear a shirt and tie to vote. Let's just put it out there: get rid of that law so that Republicans can legally institute methodologies to impede minority-voting.

Racist politicians (at least in Texas for now if this passes) will no longer have to pander to people they don't care about. They can simply create all sorts of rules and requirements that will deter AMS from coming to the polls and address the people that they really care about. After all, white folks have done enough for AMS; bringing them out of the jungle, enslaving them, feeding them scraps of food, messing up their families by raping their queens, freeing them without giving them a pot to urinate in, giving AMS second-class jobs to remain as second-class citizens for as long as possible; incarcerating AMS for spitting on the sidewalk; offering some of us a fair education, and then, talking about AMS for putting us in a condition of need. Master...I mean, we should be so glad for all that mainstream America has done for us and against us; so, if the Republicans fear AMS voting, we should not vote. No, because of what they have done we should vote in great numbers no matter what Voter ID laws are prevalent. We truly learned how to pray and believe that only the God of the universe could bring continuance, meaningful change.

For this, the country pays. Inge Marler, the leader of the Tea Party in Arkansas, made a statement on June 14, 2012, that some will find offensive, and divisive; but the lead-in joke served its purpose as many laughed.

In the joke, a black kid asks his mother, "what's a democracy?" and the mother proceeds to answer in broken, slave-driven English, that it is when (example) 'po white folks' work for black people to receive benefits. It probably is funnier to white folks with heightened slave-driven English with a few "sho'nuffs" thrown in. Funny how insensitive white folks never relate to the fact that the joke only has relevance because of the cruelty of white folks who made it against the law for black folks to read and write. I know this is 2012 so where is my sense of humor?

Evil does not go away; it simply takes another form. We never addressed the cold, calculating, political shenanigans of the late President Ronald Reagan. He used the racist code words "state rights" in the South to win approval; along with regulation, reduced government spending, and strong anti-Soviet policies. He cut many social programs that were in place to straighten out some of the missteps of our great democracy. Republicans have elevated him to hero status and AMS sit around wondering what in the world is going on? Are we talking about the same man? It has been his regime of deregulation that has led to the financial crisis that decimates this country in 2007-2012. We pray for relieve soon.

The spiritual word, 'soul,' encompasses the part of a human being that develops, sustains, and frames thought, emotions, and actions for personal and corporate responses. Souls are always being called upon to think and emote and to align varied abstract concepts into corresponding actions.

As a country, we have assisted many countries and it cannot be denied that all we have assisted have needed our help. It can be said that Israel has fought to become a state for generations, and the soul of the country has persevered. However, it has persevered by possession. Jewish people entered a region and basically remained there. Some can say because of their presence, the region flourished and more Jews and Arabs moved into the region. Eventually, the Jewish people were in a position to declare, develop, and sustain a Jewish state. It is a lesson learned as the United States allows more people with stronger convictions than our laws can even support, to move into this country and practice with passion their own beliefs, at a time when we have no soul. In other words, a country with a flexible set of mores and moral standards is bound to search for its soul and a better way of spiritual living. With passionate people in place with passionate spiritual beliefs, they will serve as the standard. Marginalize Christianity and Catholicism all we want and this country will pay. It is not out of the question to believe that one day we will have to deal with what we allow, the good, bad, and the ugly.

June 19, 2014

It has been a series of controversies surrounding the decision-making of President Barack Obama regarding military intervention in foreign countries. In Benghazi, Libya, on September 11, 2012, an attack was launched on the United States Diplomatic Mission and several US citizens were killed. The question arose whether there was prior intelligence on the attack and if not there should have been sense it was on the anniversary date of 911. Remember this event.

Today, the President conducted a press conference about whether the United States would send troops to help squash the rebellion in Iraq led by the terrorist faction ISIS. A common thread runs through these complicated situations. In Benghazi, human bureaucracies often fail to communicate properly in all situations and people die; especially when we have no business being in certain places. In Iraq, the battle has been going on for thousands of years and we can't end it. It is about religious commitment and our country can't really understand such powerful ideologies.

Each situation provides an opportunity to reflect in hindsight and to question the decision-making of the President. Yet, the continuous questioning simply reveals our flaws. We are a powerful democracy until we elect a president of color; then, we become a bunch of petty school boys trying to show who is the biggest bully.

The country and its ideologies lose credibility and the Republican Party is so busy doing their best to sabotage the man that they cannot see the damage being done to the country and its international image. In short, if the country's leadership cannot respect and honor the man who hold the title as President, why should any other country? And if countries around the world don't respect the man, America no longer appears capable of stopping any country's conflict.

Race and the General Welfare
August 22, 2010

Dr. Laura Schlesinger's radio program allowed her the unmitigated gall to say the N-word 11 times and to state that African Americans can say it so why can't others. Stupid question that crosses cultural and racial boundaries (she's Jewish I think). But she offended on several fronts: one she used a word that is extremely negative and her caller was a black woman married to a white man. Poor listener and fan of Dr. Laura: she was concerned about her husband's friends talking about her because of her race. Dr. Laura did not service a loyal caller to her own radio show simply because she wanted her moment to air her previously hidden racist agenda. Instead of apologizing without strings attached, she turns the whole issue into a case of First Amendment Rights. Duh? After the Civil Rights Movement, Dr. Laura, white folks can't go on the air and spread outright racist remarks. She slipped up and forgot the program that has been so carefully laid by Hannity, Limbaugh, and Beck: As long as your racist comments are not overt, and are politically-based, you can stir the waters of racism as much as you like and increase listeners.

I really don't appreciate how blacks and whites say that slavery is over so get over it. Dr. Laura made a reference to this point in her bitter discourse with the woman listener who happened to be AMS and married to a white man. But I remember Daddy getting harassed on the waters of Kissimmee River and he lifted his rifle up and cocked it to show that he wasn't going to take it. Then a few years later, I remember how he turned sheepishly away after the white gas station attendant called him boy and told him to get away from here we don't allow niggers to use the restroom (going through Georgia on the way to DC.) My father finished the seventh grade and my mother finished the fourth because they spent time during season picking cotton or apples, or whatever. Blacks had split sessions in which they were actually allowed out of school to harvest crops and to plant the next season.

And if you go back to slavery, it was dangerous to read and write because such a Negro would be able to ascertain where he or she was located and might be able to escape. Our language was primarily learned by sound so we shortened some words and lengthened others and came up with derivatives of others as we communicated to others our interpretation of the words. We ate the food tossed aside by the master and they were the less meaty parts of the animal. We still eat oxtails, pig intestines (chitterlings or chitlins), pig feet and chicken necks which to me is a nuisance and waste of time because of the little meat one finds. We learned to make due with less; we made due by being frugal; we made due emotionally by learning not to complain; whatever state I am in I have learned to be content. We called ourselves the racist, derogatory name given to us by the oppressive American culture; and now our youth sing the word in songs.

Well, that's good for a lesson in perseverance but having no culture to use as a standard, all of the aforementioned became our slave culture; we have a culture of lack and of pain. Those who attained a greater understanding and some material wealth had to be looked upon to fulfill the needs of close relatives and the community alike. Their economic status gave them more choices in where they could live and how they could live. Prior to the Civil Rights Movement, bankers and teachers lived next to janitors and migrant workers.

Most slaves were used to produce sugar, the most labor intensive of the money-making crops grown in the New World. The rest of the slaves were used to produce familiar staples that have graced the Fortune 30 today: coffee, tobacco, and cotton. People who cry socialism today (accusing an African-American president of Marxism) should note the irony that the infamous (or great, depending on your politics) Karl Marx declared that turning Africa into a breeding ground for slaves for the purpose of maintaining labor for the accumulation of wealth marked the "rosy dawn of capitalism."

Some geniuses decided to return stolen land to the Native Americans; give Japanese-Americans millions of dollars for internment during WWII; and give German-Jewish survivors of the Holocaust 500 million dollars just because we didn't save them from the horrific slaughter. We, of the generous nation, came up with affirmative action to compensate former slaves and it is and was deemed unconstitutional. It was another way of looking like the master was still looking out for the children of slaves. Our pain lasted longer, deeper, and created a culture of oppression. Once freed, AMS still fueled the capitalist machinery by filling in those low paying, low-qualifications- positions that Mexican people now hold. In a social caste system, AMS have been replaced from being on the bottom socially but we have not been redeemed economically.

There was a way to put the economic inequality behind us but that would have allowed equal competition for a capitalistic future. The clean break was in the forty acres and a mule that Sherman briefly enacted for the freed slaves. The clean break was with some type of restitution such as that which occurred with the Jews, Japanese, and Native Americans.

But why not provide restitution for former slaves? Even free college tuition for twenty years or tax free living for twenty years; would have provided a better resolution than having a racist society dole out jobs or unconstitutional quotas under the stigma of giving something that was undeserved.

Worst of all, soon after slaves were freed, the commonsense approach was disavowed and little was done. Capitalistic white folks conspired to take advantage of a niche market: desperate, uneducated former slaves. Freed slaves still provided low-wage and free labor. Some still were slaves after being given freedom. And some were allowed to succeed; but if too many succeeded, that would confirm the brutality, contempt, and insecurity of the former oppressor.

Some white folks watched over former slaves; giving them jobs and being kind-hearted but in a sense, they were taking AMS out of the free-market, unlimited capitalistic system because their success was regulated by the former oppressor. Successful AMS were threatened, had their land taken, or lynched. When blacks were successful jockeys they took us off the horses; and as golf purses increased tremendously, the PGA tour showcases two or less black caddies.

No, Dr. Laura; unfortunately no way we can get over racism right now because it's still working against us and benefiting unsympathetic, disrespectful, greedy people like you.

August 1, 2013

The Philadelphia Eagles are a good football team (some would argue) that has to deal with an unfortunate situation caused in part by the racist socio-economic structure in America. Riley Cooper is a wide receiver and a 3-year veteran who called an AMS security guard the n-word. Now, in high school, the sport of football (in my southern upbringing) had a fair amount of rednecks and racists but usually they were contained to lineman and a few linebackers; usually the big and tough crew. Surprisingly, the racist comments have come from the skill positions: quarterbacks and wide receivers.

To be honest and fair (black folks always want to be fair), I think most people born in the last thirty years (1983) have experienced the full cultural indoctrination of hearing the n-word in popular music and school conversations; especially, if they listen to rap.

Caucasian males who grew up listening to this music have been inundated with the n-word in the music and have sang powerful lyrics that have signified their toughness and competitiveness. That doesn't mean that I am giving a free pass to use the n-word for white males who grew up with rap but it does mean that I have to consider how popular, culturally-based music, may color and skew the backdrop for ethnic, socio-economic, and political, opinions.

Commonsense must still prevail. Riley Cooper was attending a country music concert and I am sure he felt empowered being around so many of his friends; apparently someone close to him videotaped him. In his empowerment, and being at a place which had probably few minorities, he called one of the few minorities the n-word.

Stating the obvious, he strategically thought out and uttered highly emotional, derogatory comments in a place where he felt comfortable. But he works in a place filled with people who have been victimized by the characterization of his racist word. If he had not been at a country music concert, I would have desired to be fair and support forgiveness for his "mistake."

Another reason why it is ridiculous to use the n-word in music; with songs blaring along the highways and byways advertising a powerful epithet that record moguls have decided to encourage Americans to embrace.

Sandy Hook and Gun Control

On December 14, 2012, a crazed, young man walked into Sandy Hook Elementary School in Newton, Connecticut, and killed twenty children and six adults. Prior to this heinous act, he killed his mother in their Newtown home. His mother was a lover of various forms of guns and had taken her son to the shooting range with her.

As America was inundated with the innocent, white faces of the victims, the gun control issue raised its ugly head. What appears as common sense for African-Americans oddly but not surprisingly, conflicts with the desires of the majority. Assault rifles such as the one the killer Adam Lanza used, need to be banned. High volume ammunition clips such as the ones used by drug-dealers in our communities should be banned. The issue moved to the forefront when white kids were killed; but black kids have been getting killed for decades.

August 28, 2010 the Glenn Beck Rally March on Washington
This is getting sicker and sicker. Glenn Beck has a dream and on the date of Martin Luther King's "I Have a Dream" speech, Mr. Beck chose to have a rally at the Lincoln Memorial. Unfortunately, thousands attended as well as the niece of Dr. King.

September 9, 2013

In September 2013, NAACP leader Ben Jealous announced he would leave the position in December. He has been a model for young AMS leadership in the country. He has been extremely political and has towed the liberal, Democratic line with little regard to real needs of the AMS community.

In a political effort to keep the status quo during a period of a slow economic downturn, Democrats upped the ante and ignored the debate for jobs and focused on gay rights. Suddenly, a party that had been politically thwarted by the Republicans and the Tea Party, became a viable worldwide enforcer for the rights of homosexuals. It is not that the homosexual issue didn't need to be addressed, but it was prioritized ahead of jobs and economic development.

Dr. Boyce Watkins, professor at Syracuse University, reveals some of the relevant facts that complicate our view of leadership and the organizational purpose of the NAACP.

The AMS community benefits from the organization's defense of voter's rights and various civil rights issues but in 2013, the question arises as to the blurred moral lines surrounding the organization's survivability. The organization has survived but at what cost? Dr. Boyce Watkins writes in his article, "Ben Jealous Leaving the NAACP May Not Mean Much for Black People," about the great job Mr. Jealous has done to extricate the historical organization from its financial woes of the past.

The AMS in my circles have questioned how does the NAACP survive with little or no drives or grassroots requests for financial assistance. Dr. Watkins reminds us of the strange economic bedfellows secured by the NAACP in the form of the Wells Fargo Bank. He reminds us of donations by the bank to the NAACP; the bank which "did more to steal the homes of black people than the KKK ever did." Wells Fargo was a leader of predatory lending in the AMS community.

Assuming such an alliance crossed the boundaries of moral principles for businesses, it can be contended that other such alliances exist, and these alliances have helped to get the NAACP in the black.

Was Ben Jealous wrong or was he merely making due with limited resources to accomplish a financial goal? The blurred lines of leadership have to be redefined. All corporate entities have civic and social responsibilities and it can be stated that the NAACP has greater of these type of responsibilities than most organizations. Is the NAACP a branch of the Democratic Party, especially when we have an AMS President or a prominent AMS political official? Or do we owe so much to generations of oppressed people that we must guard the appearance of "sleeping with the enemy?"

It is really not that simple. The organization should be allowed to take monies from various organizations but absent of misguided governance. Taking money and being slack for years on community priorities is a crime of sorts. What are the initiatives of the historical black organization? Have they been forgotten among a strictly liberal agenda that in the past has been aligned with the AMS community?

The new leader of the NAACP must dust off the constitution of the organization and renew a commitment to its own priorities. If any organization was prepared to make the Democratic Party stick to its economic policies, it would have been the NAACP. Who stands up for the AMS community when politics turns the two-headed beast that is American political system?

AMS Keeps Paying---The O'Donnell Heights Murders

The young killer, handcuffed, and getting into the police cruiser, said: "You woulda thought we killed the President or something..."

It is vital to our community that we create, develop, and nurture standards that will be passed down from generation to generation. As we have developed and seek to develop a sense of community post-slavery, post-Jim Crow, and post-Civil Rights fighting, specific standards have to be addressed. After all, many of our communities evolve from past atrocities interpreted in the shadow of various housing projects throughout the country. The street mentality is really a survivalist mentality that has flourished in communities that have sought to maintain some form of dignity. Everything is connected and popular albeit negative behaviors tend to have a strong impact. We need to revisit community standards and insist that they are observed. The statement above saddened me coming from a young man who had murdered five women. The following story depicts events that led to this heinous crime.

On December 5, 1999, it was quite a story; the slaughter of innocent people; and worst of all, the slaughter of women. We didn't know just how innocent they were but we knew that it was more than likely that women involved in the kind of mischief that got people killed were probably placed in that position by men. It is difficult for people to understand how AMS feel. We visit relatives, or restaurants, or seek entertainment in neighborhoods that envelope the highest murder rate in the land. We live with the risk so much that it becomes an expectation that someone we know in a specific age range will be killed.

O'Donnell Heights broke all the rules. We attend churches and sell products in communities that we refuse to leave behind. We return for soul food and for that special seamstress that no department store can match. We learn to not expect trouble although the risks increase with each visit; the odds are sure to catch up with us as we mingle. Visiting becomes a consideration of how much risk am I willing to take; so, quite naturally, some of us simply learn how to distance ourselves from favorite friends and relatives still living in the hood.

Some facts regarding the O'Donnell Heights housing project come from an article, December 12, 1999, by Peter Hermann and Tim Craig, entitled: "Drugs and violence claim their own turf. "

The O'Donnell Heights housing project was the second largest in Baltimore in terms of land. It's integrated with more than 2000 residents in 800 dwellings. The AMS community used to say that housing projects were built with a specific design and in certain locations to facilitate humility and conquest if a revolt occurs. They are also perfectly-suited for the drug culture; with great numbers of a niche market stacked upon each other. The average family income is only $5400 a year, and this income arrives in a timely fashion near the first of the month. Elevators don't work to control people traffic. Phone lines are cut to prevent calls to the police. Outside cable boxes are opened to hide cocaine and this disrupts service. Lights are shot out because drug dealers and users like the dark.

The housing projects break the conventions of American society in that the people of our communities want to feel safe and experience a modicum of confidence in their neighbors; and in receiving assistance if something goes wrong. In these communities, our people still attend the local churches and some quietly pray and aspire that God will change the community or move the church to the suburbs. Society appears to have grown accustomed to African-Americans killing themselves; but the people in these communities refuse to live without hope. They are the individuals of the families who experience disaster after disaster; they live in the aftermath of internal chaos and they navigate its tentacles without fear because it is the only life they know. All AMS is aware of these community variables; so, we know what is probable and possible when we hear the news reports. The victim most likely is a black male, living in the city, between the ages of 13-26; and most likely connected to the drug trade in some way.

Thank God that people in these communities still go to church. Unfortunately, the killings occurred on a Sunday. Ironic that flowers of life were destroyed on a day that honors life in our communities; a sacred day for many. I can imagine some lost souls saying: "Let's rob the drug-house and kill some women on Sunday because that's a great day for honoring peace and quiet."

Gunmen made their way to the 3500 block of Elmley Ave., in Belair-Edison, to score drug money and a package of cocaine. When it was all over, they had very little by any standard, while taking the lives of five women. Police say the slaying of a male relative that night near a city school was linked to the case.

Col. John Gavrilis, said in a televised Dec. 6 press conference, that the five women inside the house on Elmley Ave. were "killed to make a statement" in an ongoing drug war in the southeastern Baltimore neighborhood of O'Donnell Heights, from which all of the victims hailed. According to Ronald McNeil, who witnessed the slayings and whose mother, sister, and niece were killed, and other sources, one of the victims was a direct target of killers who wanted to steal her drug stash and money.

Gavrilis, head of the department's Criminal Investigations Bureau (which includes the Homicide Unit), said the house "was used for drug activity," but that the victims were unaware of it and were killed to send a message to those involved in the trafficking. "The people involved were saying, 'You need to fear us. If you don't do business the way we want it done, we will kill you,'" the colonel said.

207

Police said the residence accounted for selling about 2 pounds of cocaine a day. It did not appear to be a drug rivalry but an opportunity that a customer and associate of the family wanted to seize. It doesn't matter how tough or ruthless the woman, most thugs look down on having a woman or women front their gangster enterprises. The thieves could reflect upon the weakness of having women run such a risky, dangerous venue, but they could not connect to real motherhood; only the kinds of mothers that they had seen.

The women were identified as Mary McNeil Matthews, 39, who owned the house; Levanna Spearman, 23; Mary Helen Collien, 56; Makisha Jenkins, 18; and Trennell Alston, 26. Collien is Matthews' mother and Jenkins' grandmother. Mary McNeil, the mother of Makisha Jenkins, owned the house and sold drugs along with her male companion. They also kept drug money in the house. The grandmother of Makisha and mother of Mary Mcneil Matthews, Mary Helen Collien, was reported to have rented cars for drug dealers. Levanna rented a basement room and Trennell was a family friend who lived in the community. The latter two women were family friends who were cousins by marriage. Spearman was dating another of Matthews' children, Tavaris McNeil, 22, who also was killed the same day in a separate attack. Alston was dating Ronald McNeil's son.

If there ever was a case of the impact of not snitching it was this. Friends and cousins don't snitch; here they died. Neighbors don't get involved and don't snitch; here one died. And one or two of the ladies may have known nothing about what was really going on in the house; it's always a possibility that someone dies without a clue, innocent of the crime. The odd thing is that criminals in the community, drug dealer wannabes and users alike, knew what was going on at that residence. Their secret world spilled over and took the lives of women and everyone knows that you just don't kill women. There is no honor among the new lawbreakers. They haven't counted the cost of losing potential during desperate times for renewal and regeneration.

The sixth victim, Tavaris McNeil, 22, who also lived with his mother, Mary McNeil Matthews, at the Elmley Avenue house, was dating Levanna Spearman. His body was found a day later, Monday morning. He had been shot and killed on a school playground in Northeast Baltimore, on Goodnow Road. Unfortunately, his body was discovered by some innocent children walking to school. One of the suspects was found by police lying on a sidewalk with his throat slashed.

On December 6, 1999

Police arrested one man and continued searching for three others in the execution-style shootings of the five women. Ismael Malik Wilson, 27, of the 1200 block of Gusryan St. in O'Donnell Heights, was charged with five counts of first-degree murder and was being questioned last night by homicide detectives.Police said the victims -- including a grandmother, her daughter and granddaughter -- were not involved with drugs, but were relatives or friends of suspected dealers and were targeted by a rival group who wanted to send a deadly message.

On December 9, 1999

An extensive manhunt for a suspect wanted in one of Baltimore's worst mass killings ended at a Jessup motel on U.S. 1. Heavily armed police acted on a tip and discovered the alleged murderer in the parking lot at the roadside lodging. Jessup is the town that houses one of Maryland's premiere maximum security prisons. Tavon McCoy, 21, is the third person to be arrested in Sunday's killings of five women in a Northeast Baltimore rowhouse. He is charged with five counts of first-degree murder and was being held without bail at the Central Booking and Intake Center. Police and federal marshals were searching for a fourth man, Robert Bryant, 23, of the 1200 block of Cavendish Way in O'Donnell Heights, a public housing community in Southeast Baltimore.

Tavon McCoy, 21, is the third person to be arrested in Sunday's killings of five women in a Northeast Baltimore rowhouse. He is charged with five counts of first-degree murder and was being held without bail last night at the Central Booking and Intake Center.

Police and federal marshals were searching for a fourth man, Robert Bryant, 23, of the 1200 block of Cavendish Way in O'Donnell Heights, a public housing community in Southeast Baltimore.

Burial arrangements

The arrest of McCoy comes as the victims' families are completing burial plans. Funerals are scheduled today and tomorrow in Baltimore, and on Sunday in North Carolina, where four members of one family will be laid to rest in a single afternoon.

Three men—Ismael Malik Wilson, 27; his brother Tariq Malik, 20; and Tavon McCoy, 21—have been arrested and charged in the murders. At press time police were still searching for a fourth suspect, Robert Bryant, 23.

City Paper submitted a list of questions to Gavrilis' office Dec. 10 regarding his characterization of the killings. He had not responded as of press time.

Ronald McNeil—Mary McNeil-Matthews' brother and Mary Collien's son—said in an interview that he was in the Elmley Avenue house with Jenkins, Spearman, and Alston when the suspects arrived, having kidnapped McNeil and McNeil-Matthews' brother Alvin Thomas and driven to the house in Thomas' girlfriend's car. (Police sources say Thomas was severely beaten around the head during the incident.) The men brought Thomas to the front door at gunpoint and demanded to be let in, says McNeil (who acknowledges that he had been using marijuana before the killers arrived). Once they got in, one of them took Thomas back to the car and remained there.

When the men discovered that McNeil-Matthews wasn't home, they ordered someone in the house to call her and tell her to return, McNeil says. When she did, accompanied by her mother, the men demanded her stash and money, he says, quoting one of the suspects as saying, "Give up the shit, or it's gonna cost you." McNeil says his sister—calling the men, whom she knew, by their street names—told them she didn't have any drugs or money in the house at the time. He says the men then herded everyone in the house into a basement and ransacked the house, emptying drawers and closets, pulling out sofa cushions, and even looking in a crawlspace in a rear bedroom. Failing to find anything, they demanded, "Where's the stuff? Where's the stuff?" McNeil says. He says his sister told them someone else had it.

McNeil says his mother was sent upstairs into the kitchen with one of the men while he and the four other women remained in the basement, with two of the men holding them with a shotgun and a .9 mm handgun. He says he was lying on a waterbed in the room. At some point, he says, it seemed to him as if the gunmen received a signal from the man in the kitchen. "I heard all these popping sounds. . . . They started shooting," he says, sweeping his arm to take in the whole room. All the women were shot in the head, but McNeil says he was only grazed in the elbow: "How he missed me, to this day I don't know."

McNeil says he lay across the bed, covered with his sister's and niece's blood, and played dead as the gunmen went upstairs. He then heard another, single gunshot, and the men leaving the house, he says.

"I lay perfectly still for at least five minutes," McNeil says, then he ventured upstairs and found his mother lying on the kitchen floor, also shot in the head. He says that as he called 911, he heard his mother breathing, but then the breathing stopped. He then banged on a neighbor's door and asked them to call 911.

Although police sources agree with McNeil about the motive for the crime, they say the investigation has cast doubt on some elements of his account of the shooting. Sources say the wounds the women suffered were not consistent with open fire as described by McNeil, but from guns pressed against their heads. Sources also say there was relatively little blood on the scene, indicating the victims died instantly (and their hearts stopped pumping blood), which would have been less likely if the gunmen opened fire in the manner described by McNeil.

At the trial, it was mentioned that Ronald McNeil had gun residue on his hand. But the jury did not hear:

What the jury did not hear was that McNeil is charged with murder in the apparent revenge killing in January 2000 of Chris Manning, 22.

Or that, court records show, he was charged with threatening the mother of his child and trying to get her to lure his brother-in-law to her house so he could "do him" in revenge for the Elmley killings.

Or that he spent 15 years in a Florida prison for murdering his grandfather in 1984.

Police sources say Alvin Thomas escaped during a botched meeting between the suspects and another man in the 2800 block of Greenmount Avenue, which the suspects apparently arranged by phone. Sources say the meeting was to have taken place at 28th Street and Greenmount, but the man whom the suspects had called sensed something was wrong as he approached the appointed place, and continued driving another block to a McDonald's. The man ran inside the restaurant, followed by one of the alleged killers, whose gun was drawn. An off-duty school police officer who was working as a security guard fired a shot at the armed man, who escaped back to the car with the other suspects and drove away. Police sources say the man who had entered the restaurant initially claimed the suspects had tried to carjack him, but later acknowledged being contacted by the suspects.

Later the same night, several residents of a garden-apartment complex in the 4900 block of Goodnow Road called police to say they had heard gunshots. Police investigated but couldn't see anything unusual, police sources say. At 7:45 A.M. on Dec. 6, children on their way to school found the body of McNeil-Matthews' 22-year-old son, Tavares McNeil, lying at the side of an apartment building, his body hidden from the street by a row of hedges. Police have not publicly linked that killing with the shootings at Elmley Avenue or charged anyone in Tavares McNeil's murder.

Despite his sister's involvement in drugs, Ronald McNeil says, she wasn't in any way a violent person. Family members begged her to get a gun for protection, he says, but she refused: "She wouldn't have a gun in her house."

A first-degree murder warrant has been issued for Ronald P. McNeil, 37, of the 3500 block of Elmley Ave. in Belair-Edison, where the five drug-related killings occurred Dec. 5.

The warrant contends he shot and killed Chris Manning, 22, about noon Jan. 25 at O'Donnell Street and Demarcay Way.

McNeil has been in the Baltimore jail since a shootout Feb. 3 with police at the Elmley Avenue home. McNeil's mother, sister and niece were among the five women killed in the house when four gunman opened fire when they could not find a 2.2-pound package of cocaine they were seeking.

Two family friends also were killed in the home and, the next morning, McNeil's nephew was found dead behind a nearby elementary school.

On Feb. 3, police were trying to serve McNeil with a false imprisonment arrest warrant, alleging he kidnapped a woman and forced her at gunpoint to phone his brother-in-law and lure him to the Elmley Avenue home.

"Get him over here, so I can do him," McNeil told the woman, according to a statement of charges filed in Baltimore District Court. The woman has been identified as Priscilla Harrison.

When the brother-in-law refused, McNeil threatened the woman's family, police said. "If you breathe a word to this to anyone, I know where your family lives," he said, according to charging documents.

McNeil stood accused of firing four shots at police.

Police officials, who have never fully explained the December shooting, would not say a day earlier how Manning might have been connected to the carnage in the Elmley Avenue home. Cook-Hayes said police never considered Manning a suspect. However, Manning lived in the 6100 block of Toone St. in O'Donnell Heights, a community where the massacre suspects and some of the victims first became acquainted.

Four men, connected to an O'Donnell Heights drug gang, were indicted last month on murder charges in the shooting of the women.

McNeil -- convicted of assault with intent to murder in 1993 and sentenced to six years in prison -- has told reporters that he witnessed the five slayings and escaped by playing dead as the gunmen opened fire on the women, some of whom were sitting next to him in the basement of the home.

A week after the killings, McNeil gave television news crews a tour of the bloodstained house and recounted how he survived. Police have neither confirmed nor rebutted his story.

He continued to live in the house until his arrest.

Lack of Concern

The funeral was held in Whiteville, North Carolina. Mary Alice McNeil, the 77-year-old matriarch of a family now scattered from Orlando, Fla., to Los Angeles, tearfully watched funeral services for her daughter, granddaughter and two great-grandchildren. Not all were born here, but McNeil said this is their home. A reminder of the contrasts in lifestyles; slow southern living to the hustle and bustle of the northern anxieties. We all have to return home one day.

More than 300 mourners packed the Brunswick-Waccamaw

Missionary Baptist Association hall

Mary McNeil's eldest of 11 children, Mary Helen Collien, 56, was shot dead in the kitchen. Her granddaughter, Mary McNeil Matthews, 39, and her great-granddaughter Makisha Jenkins, 18, were shot while lying on a basement bed along with two friends. The friends, Lavanna Spearman, 23, and Trennell Alston, 26, were buried Friday and Saturday in Baltimore.

The lack of concern from Baltimore's elected officials for its citizens disappoints and bewilders me.

Their scant concern expressed was about the impact of the deaths on the city's reputation, rather than on the victims of the crime.

Murder Trial

Each of the four men is charged with five counts of first-degree murder and faces life in prison if convicted.

The mass killing was the worst in Baltimore in more than a decade. It became national news, and was the subject of a true-crime television show; and it symbolized the city's lethal drug wars that terrorize entire neighborhoods.

"There are no warm and cuddly people in this one," William B. Purpura, who represents McCoy, said in an interview. "It is complicated. It's a mess."

McNeil, 37, told police and reporters at the time that he was in the basement of the house when men opened fire there. The women killed included his mother, sister and niece. He survived, he said at the time, by playing dead.

In opening statements to the jury yesterday, defense lawyers suggested McNeil, who emerged unhurt from the house, could have been one of the killers, instead of their clients.

They noted that ballistics testing found McNeil had gunshot residue on both hands, probably transferred there by firing a gun.

Did the defendants simply miss McNeil, who was lying on a basement bed with two of the women, as they opened fire, asked Arcangelo M. Tuminelli, Bryant's lawyer. "I submit to you, that's not real plausible," Tuminelli said.

"My biggest concern is that a citizen comes across one of these guys and ends up in the cross-fire between people out for revenge," said Col. John E. Gavrilis, chief of the detective bureau.

A second suspect, Ismael Malik Wilson, 27, who was arrested Monday night, was ordered held yesterday without bail. "If it could be higher, I'd make it higher," said District Judge Timothy J. Doory, noting the suspect's long list of arrests and two felony convictions.

Police are struggling to determine a motive for the shootings of the women -- including one age 56, her daughter and granddaughter -- at the Elmley Avenue rowhouse in Northeast Baltimore. The shooting of a male relative near a city school the same night has been linked to the horrific irresponsible indulgence.

Investigators have said the women were not involved with drugs but were friends or relatives of dealers in O'Donnell Heights, and were killed by rival dealers to send a deadly message. Yesterday, police sources offered two theories about what prompted one of the city's worst mass killings:

The shooters were after a 2.2 pound package of cocaine worth up to $28,000 on the street -- or they had been stiffed on a drug shipment. Police sources said that up to 2 pounds of cocaine was sold from Elmley Avenue each day.

While most of Baltimore's 300-plus homicides each year are linked to the city's entrenched drug trade, the execution-style shootings of five women in a single home shocked veteran detectives and all who heard of it.

Keep On Paying

A 17-year-old AMS youth pleaded guilty in Baltimore Circuit Court to the Oct. 20, 1989, murder and robbery of a popular Baltimore schoolteacher. The criminal opportunity began to take shape when a friend suggested robbing someone to get money to buy cocaine.

Derrick Antonio Allbrook faced a maximum penalty of life plus 40 years for killing Jerome C. McDaniel, who taught at Ashburton Elementary School. He was scheduled to be sentenced Jan. 29 by Judge Ellen M. Heller.

His guilty plea resolves one of three cases pending against Allbrook, who also is charged with an armed robbery and with another murder, in December 1988. That murder, allegedly committed with Timothy Maurice Jones, 19, also occurred in Druid Hill Park under circumstances similar to Mr. McDaniel's murder, the police said.

The AMS youth often have no sense of how respect or the lack thereof, impacts our communities.

January 21, 2008

In Winnfield, Louisiana, Baron Pikes was chased after being under suspicion of cocaine possession. Baron Pikes was the first-cousin of Mychal Bell from the Jena Six school boys who were arrested during racial tensions involving an ongoing high school conflict. A national furor took place and civil rights leaders from across the country traveled to Louisiana. Mr. Pikes, age 21, was chased and apprehended near a small shopping area downtown. He was asked to get up and either couldn't or refused to do so. Instead of a couple of officers grabbing him and tossing him in the cruiser,

Officer Scott Nugent tased Mr. Pikes while he was in handcuffs, with two other officers standing nearby. The point is three officers should have been able to lift, toss, and subdue the young suspect. His death certificate reads that he was tased twice while unconscious. He was tased a total of nine times. You would think that someone would have crossed that old blue racist line and made the brilliant suggestion: "Hey, let's lift him up and put him in the cruiser."

Mr. Pikes is dead and Scott Nugent has been fired. A greater, more deep-seated evil still exists. The police department lied and stated that Mr. Pikes told them he was on drugs and had asthma. I guess this would explain why he died after improper police procedures. Huh? Fact is no drugs were found in his system; he didn't have asthma; and it really wouldn't have mattered. Clouding the issue is another method that corrupt police officers and departments use to escape public scrutiny and punishment: He was a drug addict; he skipped school; he was previously arrested. These guys are morally inadequate to have a job as police officers. Most people are missing the point: what happens when married cops discriminate against single mothers, or large women, or women with short-shorts or tight dresses? People who live with the ignorance of racial prejudice in their hearts generally carry more than one type of prejudice.

Death While In Custody
February 16, 2010

Death while in custody is a common way that some officers allegedly take out their frustration with criminals who have committed a grave wrong; such as trying to get away. These reckless officers weaken the justice system at its most basic and observable lesson and people rightfully question whether they can trust the local authorities. After an injustice is committed, it seems as if the judicial system lines up to protect governmental liability; and in doing so, the police officer is given minimal punishment, if any.

In Baltimore, the cause of death for Phillip G. Holland, 61, was stated as suicide. And it makes sense because he was found dead in his cell at the city jail on Saturday morning, around 10:30 a.m.; and no one was in the cell with him.

Mark Vernarelli, a spokesman for the state Department of Public Safety and Correctional Services reported that Mr. Holland had been taken to Johns Hopkins Hospital, where he was later pronounced dead. Mr. Vernarelli said the cause of death appeared to be suicide by asphyxiation. Internal investigators were reviewing his death.

Holland had been held since late January on multiple charges of attempted murder. On Jan. 27, officers staked out the hospital to serve a warrant on Holland, who was being sought on attempted-murder charges accusing him of stabbing a woman outside of a Hampden convenience store.

September 2011

In Richmond Heights, Missouri, Anna Brown was a homeless woman who suffered so much pain in her legs that she couldn't walk. Apparently, she was given some type of treatment and released but she still suffered in pain. Ms. Brown was 29 years of age and an AMS woman. She had visited several hospitals during the day of her death and had received painkillers from one. But she knew that something more serious was wrong. She refused to leave the emergency room and the police arrested her for trespassing and took her to jail. They assumed that she was on drugs. After being in jail for a few minutes, her problem was ended...she died.

July 16, 2012

In Dayton, Ohio, Kylen English was 20 years-old and riding in a police cruiser. Mr. English had been arrested because he was attempting to kick in the door of the aunt of his 16-year-old girlfriend. The aunt called the police to protect her niece from Kylen English. Law enforcement says that he broke the window of the cruiser while in handcuffs and jumped off the Salem Avenue Bridge. Now the people have gained access to a Montgomery County Jail video that shows Kylen walking into the jail and collapsing to the floor. Conveniently, the coroner's office has ruled the death a suicide. Huh? The FBI has opened a civil rights investigation into the incident.

Morally corrupt cops who commit illegal and deadly acts against AMS are also usually liars. When you weigh the odds, you can't blame them. They can admit that they have done a dastardly deed and lose their jobs and possibly go to prison or they can lie and run the risk of losing their jobs and going prison. With no enactment of serious penalties for cops who commit perjury, it is apparently a risk worth taking.

July 17, 2014

A police officer on Staten Island, New York, placed a very large man in an illegal chokehold to subdue him for arrest. Supposedly, the man had been selling cigarettes earlier but at the time of the arrest, he was seen on video just standing. Let's keep in mind, that even if something surfaces about selling illegal cigarettes, the penalty for that crime is not death. The chokehold has been ruled illegal simply because of the fact that people have a greater chance of dying when it is administered. Smart move to render it illegal.

Mr. Garner is seen and heard on video falling to the ground and yelling: "I can't breathe, I can't breathe." Oops; perhaps the person administering the illegal hold will stop. No chance. Perhaps some fellow police officers will tell the officer to relinquish the hold. No chance. The man dies while standing on the sidewalk being black.

The American Way: Capitalism vs. Right

Michelle Obama started a campaign for fighting obesity. Sarah Palin, in her wisdom, has argued against Mrs. Obama's program by stating (paraphrased) that America can take care of itself and it does not need the government to guide it towards fixing its problems. But America needs protection against its own capitalistic ways. In a society in which fast-food companies reign and produce riches on the backs of appetites and audio- and visually-stimulated children, our children need extra support. And it is the same with various capitalistic enterprises that would not be allowed to do business in other countries because the products impede on the well-being of society. In America, we allow the product to be sold and then we pay lawyers and other institutions to fight against what most people can easily perceive as wrong; and never should have been allowed.

www.ingramcontent.com/pod-product-compliance
Lightning Source LLC
Chambersburg PA
CBHW070857290526
45795CB00001B/156